The Mindful Way

Pain Management

DR CHERYL REZEK

sheldon PRESS

First published in Great Britain in 2016

Sheldon Press
36 Causton Street
London SW1P 4ST
www.sheldonpress.co.uk

British Library Cataloguing-in-Publication Data
A catalogue record for this book is available from the British Library

ISBN 978-1-84709-421-6
eBook ISBN 978-1-84709-422-3

Typeset by Fakenham Prepress Solutions, Norfolk NR21 8NN
First printed in Great Britain by Ashford Colour Press
Subsequently digitally reprinted in Great Britain

eBook by Fakenham Prepress Solutions, Fakenham, Norfolk NR21 8NN

Produced on paper from sustainable forests

The Mindful Way
Pain Management

Dr Cheryl Rezek is a consultant clinical psychologist and mindfulness teacher who brings a fresh and dynamic approach to how mindfulness and psychological concepts can be integrated into everyone's life as a way of managing it in the most helpful way. Her work is engaging, accessible and, most importantly, realistic, and her writing easy to read and follow, giving it a broad appeal to all audiences. Her approach (affectionately known as Life Happens) is based on academic knowledge and her extensive clinical experience, and it is regarded as an emerging mindfulness-based approach. It encourages awareness of oneself within a context, the development of resilience and skills, and the use of mindfulness. She has a long-standing clinical and academic career, including working with children, adolescents and families. She has lectured, supervised, developed programmes, appeared on radio and TV shows as well as run workshops nationally and internationally.

She is the author of a number of books including *Life Happens: Waking up to yourself and your life in a mindful way* (Leachcroft); *Brilliant Mindfulness: How the mindful approach can help you towards a better life* (Pearson); *Mindfulness for Carers: How to manage the demands of caregiving while finding a place for yourself* (Jessica Kingsley); *Monkey Mind and the Mountain: Mindfulness for 8–80 year olds (and older)* (Leachcroft); *Anxiety and Depression* (Sheldon Press); and *Quit Smoking* (Sheldon Press). *Pain Management* (Sheldon Press), *Dealing with Symptoms of Cancer* (Sheldon Press) and *Grief, Loss and Loneliness* (Sheldon Press) are soon to be released. She also has a highly rated App entitled *iMindfulness on the go* (

Visit he  m>

15 349 390 5

Contents

An important note about the text

To access the audio downloads that accompany this book, go to: <www.lifehappens-mindfulness.com/book-audio>.

Do not listen to the audio material while driving or operating any machinery or item.

Disclaimer: This book makes no claim to act as a cure or treatment of any conditions, nor does it advocate discontinuation of any intervention or treatment.

Introduction

Life Happens

Life brings with it experiences and events that are some-times wonderful and at other times distressing and difficult. There may be many special moments to be had in life, but we can also find ourselves in situations where we are tested and left feeling vulnerable and frustrated. Dealing with pain is one of those harsh experiences that we all wish we didn't have to endure.

Mindfulness offers assistance by building a strong and powerful anchor within you that you can call upon when dealing with difficult experiences such as pain, whether it be low-grade or intense, acute or chronic. Pain is complex and frequently resurfaces. It can be relentless and wear you down, leading you to believe that you are powerless over it no matter what you do.

With practice and ongoing application (sadly, there is no quick fix or magic solution), developing a mindful approach will offer you an alternative solution to how you perceive and react to your pain. This approach is combined with sound psychological concepts and pain management ideas that give you a broad and inclusive framework within which to manage your pain. Another advantage of using mindfulness in your everyday life is that it increases your capacity to enjoy and appreciate your other experiences.

What use could this book be for me?

This book presents a gentle introduction to mindfulness ideas and how you can use a combination of mindfulness and psychology as an ally in coping with your pain. It will cover the different types of pain, how pain is maintained and its potential effects, as well as evidence to show how mindfulness can ease pain and the suffering that comes with it. It will lead you through each idea and mindful practice, giving you the tools to renegotiate your relationship with your pain and how to manage it now and over time.

Throughout the book, mindfulness practices are outlined and you are provided with step-by-step guidance on how to do them.

The audio of the guided practices is included as an mp3 download at <www.lifehappens-mindfulness.com/book-audio>.

When you see the symbol ◀))), it indicates that there is a guided practice that can be listened to on the audio download.

It is strongly recommended that you attempt *all* the written practices as well as those on the audio download at least once. It cannot be emphasized enough how essential and important it is that you do the practices from the audio download. Over time, you'll become more aware of which practices work best for you.

Keep in mind that doing these practices only once or twice will change very little. Engaging with them consistently is the key factor in how effective mindfulness will be for managing your pain. The more you practise, the more engrained and useful mindfulness will become in your daily life – and the greater the benefits will be.

1

Pain in perspective

Pain hurts. No matter what spin you put on it, pain is hard to tolerate and live with, especially if it is chronic. Most people have experienced some form of pain, but it is the persistent pain or pain that comes in bouts of acute intensity that can leave you feeling exhausted and despairing.

Taking control

Persistent pain wears you down to the point where you feel you have little control over your life. Chronic pain is pervasive as it seeps into all areas of your life and affects them in different ways, mostly negatively. Mindfulness makes no claim to change your life, although it can be life-changing. It is an invaluable resource that can be developed to provide you with a sense of balance and calm to draw on when life feels destructive and over-whelming, or just simply horrid. It can also enable you to be fully present in all moments whether they be of happiness and peace or of dread.

By taking the time to do the practices and by paying attention to your life, you will find that you can gain greater perspective on your pain and situation, make sense of what may seem senseless and consider choices that will bring about a feeling of well-being and balance. Importantly, this will help you to separate your physical pain from the emotional and psychological pain that is worsening your situation.

When we are in pain, it is difficult imaging being without pain, and for some people this may never be a reality. Feelings of emotional distress often develop over a long period of time and for different reasons. Giving yourself the time to be mindful of your body, and the experience it is having, can help you to control your stress and emotional reaction to the pain, which in turn can improve your emotional, psychological and physical state.

Pain hurts

Pain is defined as an uncomfortable feeling and/or an unpleasant sensation in the body that can be distressing. It is common for us to believe that pain is a reaction to an injury or a signal to us that something is wrong, either from external damage, such as stubbing a toe, or from an internal cause, such as back pain caused by overexertion or pain generated from disease. All forms of pain indicate that you should take notice.

Pain can appear suddenly or develop slowly. However, the extent to which people can tolerate the same intensity of pain depends very much on the individual, as each person has his or her own level of pain perception (the point at which the stimulus begins to hurt) and pain tolerance threshold (the point at which the person acts to stop the pain). Some people cannot bear paper cuts, whereas others can break a bone and seem to find the pain tolerable. These differences are associated with factors such as ethnicity, gender, genetics and general variations within any group.

You are not alone

- Pain is the most common reason people seek medical help.[1]
- In the UK, 5 million people develop chronic pain every year.[1]
- Only two-thirds of them will recover.[1]
- An estimated 11 per cent of adults and 8 per cent of children suffer severe pain.[2]
- Around 14 million people in the UK are estimated to suffer from all forms of chronic pain, with 13 million workdays lost to the economy each year.[3]
- In 2015, around 9.3 million workdays were lost because of work-related musculoskeletal disorders.[4]
- Pain issues in the UK are estimated to cost around £10 billion each year.[5]

- Pain in adolescents alone costs the UK £4 billion a year.[5]
- In the USA, 100 million people suffer from chronic pain.[6]
- The cost to the US economy from this is estimated to be around $600 billion a year.[6]
- Low back pain is now regarded as the leading cause of disability worldwide.[7]
- Pain in general can be so severe that 16 per cent of those suffering from chronic pain say that they have wanted to die because of it.[1]
- It is estimated that at least 1 million people in the UK are living with pain that could be better managed than it currently is.[5]

The topic of pain and its management is so widespread and diverse that there is a call to regard it as a public health issue, as well as to have it recognized as a long-term condition in its own right, separate from being secondary to a disease, disorder or syndrome.[5]

Awareness of posture

Take a moment to consider your posture as you sit and read this book, walk around the house or go about your daily routine. When you feel distressed or low in mood, you may have a tendency to slump in a chair, move more slowly, look down and have a hunched posture. If you are anxious, you may sit on the edge of a chair, move quickly and restlessly, fiddle nervously with objects or be unable to sit still for any length of time.

Emotional pain can often affect your posture in the same way as physical pain, leading you to adopt defensive or tense positions. On the other hand, when you are confident and calm, your shoulders will be held back, you will stand up straight and look ahead while walking purposefully, or sit comfortably in a chair in an upright, open and relaxed manner.

Research[8] has shown not only that your emotions affect your posture, but also that your posture can affect your emotions. By adjusting your posture, you can lift your mood, reduce aches and pains, improve blood flow around the body and increase your energy levels.

Mindfulness practice: Adjusting Posture

- Sit in a chair in a slumped and hunched position for two minutes. Become aware of your breathing and observe any sensations that come to mind. Can you feel any aches and pains? How is it affecting your breathing? What emotions can you identify?

- Now sit up straighter with your shoulders back. Your posture should be open and relaxed; try to soften your facial muscles and jaw, and nurture a feeling of confidence and calm. As you continue to focus on your breathing, notice any changes that occur either physically or emotionally. Do you feel more alert, more confident or less anxious? If no changes occur, that is fine too.

- Make a mental note of your experience, and throughout the day become aware of your posture when you feel anxious or distressed. At these times, gently and kindly adjust it if you are hunched, on the edge of your seat or sitting restlessly. Take a moment to think how these small changes may affect your physical and emotional well-being.

Pain is like a bully that dominates your thoughts, activities, mood and life. Mindfulness offers an opportunity to face the bully and manage the pain. It helps you to gain a perspective on what is happening to your life because of the pain and how you can work with, and go beyond, it. This won't cure or remove your pain, but it certainly can be enormously supportive and helpful. Perhaps the key element is that it affects and shifts your relationship to your pain.

2

The different angles of pain

We try to avoid pain by withdrawing from what is causing the pain – such as a hot stove – seeking medical help, taking medication or resting the painful area. Pain can tell you that something is wrong and encourage you to alter the situation, for example removing your hand from the hot stove, or seeking help if you don't know the cause of the pain.

Pain is not only an unpleasant sensory experience, as with the hot stove, but also an unpleasant emotional experience even if there is no medically explained cause, such as tissue or nerve damage, for the pain. Unexplained causes can create considerable emotional distress as people feel that their pain is not being regarded as real and they are not being believed.

Medically, pain is split into two categories: acute pain and chronic pain.

Acute pain

Acute pain is separate from chronic pain. When pain is labelled 'acute', it means that it is expected to last for a short time, will recover fully and is a sensation associated with a specific injury. For example, damage to parts of the body, such as the skin tissue and bones, can lead to acute pain. Acute pain begins suddenly and is usually sharp in quality. It serves as a warning of disease or a threat to the body and can be caused by many events or circumstances, including:

- surgery
- broken bones
- dental work
- burns
- cuts
- grazes
- childbirth.

Acute pain may be mild and last just a moment, or it may be severe and last longer, but it will cease after a limited time. When pain is acute, it is expected to last a maximum of 12–24 weeks (about three to six months) as this is the length of time the body may need for a minor injury to heal. The acute pain mostly disappears when its underlying cause has been treated or has healed. Unrelieved acute pain may, however, lead to chronic pain.

Acute pain often brings on a spurt of strong emotional distress, which may result in someone shouting out, losing their temper or crying.

Chronic pain

Chronic pain is pain that persists despite the fact that the injury has healed – or indeed there may have never been an injury. Unlike acute pain, it is not a warning signal of something being wrong, and therefore it does not have an important role in our survival.

The actual experience of chronic pain and the symptoms associated with it can be different from those of acute pain. Many people who live with chronic pain report symptoms such as:

- sweaty hands or palms
- sensitivity to touch (known as 'allodynia')
- changes in skin appearance (sometimes becoming scaly or pale, or losing hair)
- pins and needles
- burning
- stabbing pain
- numbness
- erratic pain
- changes in temperature
- pain that jumps around the body (moving from one spot to another)

- stiffness
- a dull ache or throbbing.

Understanding the distinction between acute and chronic pain can often be comforting, as it provides some kind of explanation for why ongoing pain is so different from the ideas we may initially have had of pain. These initial ideas about pain are that it will go away once the injury is healed, and that pain is a warning that something is wrong.

Chronic pain is a long-term form of pain. It can sometimes be brought about and maintained by a long-standing medical condition, such as multiple sclerosis or arthritis. It is often the result of damaged nerves, which can be harder to treat successfully. The ongoing or recurring nature of chronic pain can leave people frustrated and susceptible to more lasting emotional distress.

These two types of pain can both be the cause of, and be caused by, a change in our thoughts and emotions. However, the recurring and enduring nature of chronic pain poses a greater risk for causing psychological suffering, which can in turn augment the sense of pain.

Breakthrough pain

This is when pain that is usually controlled breaks through regardless of a pain management regime and medications. Approximately 70 per cent of people with chronic pain can experience this. Its cause varies but it can be due to a number of factors, such as medication wearing off over time or a seemingly random action like the everyday movement of getting out of bed.

Breakthrough pain can be intense, and it puts people at risk of feeling that their pain is immoveable and over-bearing. It may lead to feelings of helplessness, which can generate problems in other areas of people's lives, such as their work, hobbies or relationships.

Other pain categorizations

Pain can also be classified according to the type of damage that it causes. The two most common categories are pain caused by tissue damage, called nociceptive pain, and pain caused by nerve damage, referred to as neuropathic pain. There is another category referred to as psycho-genic pain; this usually arises from tissue or nerve pain, but the actual extent of pain experienced is increased or prolonged because of other factors such as stress, fear, anxiety or depression.

- Tissue damage involves injury to the body's tissues, such as bone, soft tissue or an organ, and can result from a physical injury such as a broken bone or cut, or from a disease such as cancer or arthritis. Inflammatory pain is a subcategory of pain from tissue damage, osteoarthritis being an example of this: the joints are painful, but it is the inflammatory tissue damage that causes increased pain sensitivity. Rheumatoid arthritis is also a type of inflammatory pain.

- Neuropathic pain is frequently chronic. Syndromes associated with it include, for example, central pain syndrome, complex regional pain syndrome, diabetic peripheral neuropathic pain, shingles and postherpetic neuralgia and trigeminal neuralgia.

Cancer can include a mixture of nociceptive (inflammatory) and neuropathic pain due to nerve damage, inflammation caused by treatment and tumour growth.[1] Pain can be caused by musculoskeletal, neurological, metabolic and other common disorders, such as diabetes. In addition, there is phantom pain – pain that is felt in a part of the body that has been lost so the brain is no longer actually receiving signals from it.

As mentioned above, chronic pain can also be part of other diseases, disorders or syndromes. Arthritis, osteoarthritis, cancer and multiple sclerosis are well known examples of diseases and disorders. However, syndromes (i.e. collections of signs and symptoms known to frequently appear together but without a known cause) such as fibromyalgia and irritable bowel syndrome (IBS) are also commonly associated with experiencing pain.

Pain can be caused by emotional or psychological factors, and this is sometimes referred to as the person having medically unexplained symptoms. In this situation, the pain is real but there is no specific or identifiable physical cause. Psychogenic and medically unexplained conditions can be difficult for people to understand, and the individual may be ashamed or fearful that he or she will not be believed but will be seen as in some way crazy. The fact that a physical cause cannot be identified can make people even more distressed. About one-fifth of all GP consultations in the UK are for medically unexplained symptoms.[2]

The important issue is that it's not 'all in your head'. Many individuals with symptoms such as fatigue, pain, dizziness, nausea, headaches, shortness of breath and heart palpitations also have depression or anxiety, so it is essential that the psychological component is addressed; this in turn frequently relieves many of the physical symptoms. Other factors, such as an infection or virus, may trigger syndromes like IBS or chronic fatigue, but, conversely, factors such as stress, anxiety, a serious life event or depression can trigger IBS, low back pain or chronic fatigue.

Pain is not only a physical condition but one that is affected by various factors such as emotions, socioeconomic factors and psychological and social components. Consequently, pain is no longer only the domain of the medical profession.

The physiology of pain

The medical perspective is that pain stems from sensations that are triggered in the body.

It is understood that when our nerve endings are stimulated, they take action. When we are injured, pain receptors called nociceptors are activated and shoot off a response. This electrical signal travels through the nerve, on to the spinal cord and then on to the brain. The process works at lightning speed and the signal is sent in fractions of a second.

On arrival in the brain, the pain signals are directed to several areas for interpretation and analysis. For example, parts of the cerebral cortex interpret the location of the pain and decide whether or not this is a new kind of pain you are experiencing, as your brain needs to make sense of the situation.

Signals are also sent to the emotional hub in the brain, called the limbic system. This system dictates your emotional response to pain. For example, some people will become frustrated or even irate, whereas others may cry. Associations are built over time between the physical sensations you experience and the emotions you feel.

The Gateway Theory

The Gateway Theory (or Gate Control Theory)[3] of pain says, as mentioned above, that first a situation occurs, for example a cut finger, that sends a message via nerve pathways to the central nervous system (CNS), which consists of the spinal cord and the brain. These messages travel first to the spinal cord and can then be relayed to the certain areas of the brain that analyse and interpret them. The brain sends messages back to the spinal cord with its analysis telling you you are in pain. This process by which you physically register the pain happens extremely quickly.

The pathways in the spinal cord contain what are regarded as gateways or ports. The theory holds that it is at these gateway points that pain can be renegotiated to lessen, remove or worsen it. The signals to do this come both from the body and from the brain, via the messages it has sent back. This theory also emphasizes that physical, psychological, emotional and cognitive factors can trigger or aggravate the pain you feel, but can also, when managed correctly and consistently, lessen or stop the pain.[3]

This has enormous implications for chronic pain management in terms of the factors that open the gates and the factors that close them. Factors that open the pain gates are typically as follows: stress, tension and emotional states such as anger or depression; too much focus or mental energy directed towards the pain, i.e. continually thinking or worrying about it; and lack of activity, which can lead to poor mobility, stiff joints and low levels of fitness. Factors that close the pain gateways include: activities that encourage and foster relaxation,

contentment and well-being, mental engagement in interests that make you feel involved and activities that distract
you from the pain; exercise and activity to increase your
fitness levels and help release the body's natural painkillers, as well as develop and maintain muscle tone and
joint mobility; and medications, whether prescription or
over-the-counter.[3,4]

This book looks at pain from an integrated approach
combining a biopsychosocial perspective, you as an
individual and what you bring to your pain and its management, and how a mindful framework and mindful
practices can help you through awareness, assistance
and breathing practices. These aspects will be discussed
throughout the book.

Reactions to pain

Reactions to pain can be wide-ranging depending upon
the severity of the damage. These reactions can be experienced for a short, intense period of time or can be drawn
out over many years.

What is certain is that pain is far more than sensory
and neural communications. It can be thought of as a
complex mix of personality, emotions, culture, experience, physiological sensations and responses. We can be
more vulnerable to pain depending on our genetic make-
up, our socioeconomic status and the environment in
which we live. The reaction to pain is reliant on a number

of factors as it is not a linear, one-way system of cause and effect. Your previous life experiences, current mood and beliefs about your ability to cope with pain can all play a significant role in the pain process.

As an example, consider pain in two different contexts. In the first context, you badly stub your toe shortly after hearing you have not been successful in getting a job you really wanted. In the second context, you badly stub the same toe shortly after someone you care about has just given you a gift you really appreciate. Would your reaction be exactly the same in both scenarios or would they differ?

Alternatively, what if you had once experienced a paper cut. If the last paper cut you had didn't bleed and healed quickly, you may think it is a nuisance but not feel too fearful about it happening again. However, if the last paper cut you had become infected and took a long time to heal, you're likely to feel greater emotional distress or dread if the accident repeats itself. Although these examples are relatively simple, you can see how the same injury can bring different responses based on your current situation and past experiences.

Pain is an extremely common complaint brought to physicians.[5] People turn to a physician for help if they don't know the cause of the pain and they don't believe they have the resources within themselves to heal or manage the pain they experience; essentially, they want the pain to be removed as soon as possible.

Effects of pain

Acute and chronic pain can have an effect on functioning in areas such as concentration, working memory, mental flexibility, problem solving and information processing speed.[6,7] They are also strongly associated with a host of other conditions or responses such as:

- development of mental health problems
- adverse healthcare
- poor self-care
- lower quality of life
- poorer outcome and prognosis.

Examples of these are:

- depression
- anxiety
- fear and worry
- anger
- hopelessness
- helplessness
- poor sleep
- low levels of energy
- impotence
- decrease in self-esteem, self-worth and confidence
- reduced levels of social interactions
- work-related problems through, for example, absenteeism or low productivity

- financial problems
- difficulties in maintaining social relationships
- difficulties with sexual relationships
- reduced activity and associated weight gain
- poorer eating habits
- poor physical care
- lower levels of health
- substance misuse.

A disproportionate number of people with long-term health issues and co-morbid mental health problems have more difficult socioeconomic conditions and less access to resources of all kinds.[8] People with long-term physical health conditions are the predominant users of health-care, and a large proportion of them also suffer from a range of conditions, from anxiety and depression, to dementia in older adults.[8] Up to 30 per cent of those with a physical condition develop a mental health condition, and 46 per cent of people with a mental health condition have a long-term physical condition.[8]

The research consistently reports that people with long-term conditions are two to three times more likely to experience mental health problems than the general population. People with cardiovascular disease, diabetes or chronic obstructive pulmonary disease are two to three times more likely to have depression and/or anxiety, and those with arthritis, cancer and human immuno-deficiency virus/acquired immune deficiency syndrome

(HIV & AIDS) are at least twice as likely to do so.[8] These mental health aspects mostly develop after the onset of the physical condition and frequently come about from changes in lifestyle, work, relationships, mobility and so forth, including stress, as well as from the ongoing effects of living with chronic pain. However, patients' mental health and well-being is generally overlooked and mostly goes unrecognized.

Physical conditions can lead to, or have, a very strong relationship to mental health, and it is also well documented that our psychological state contributes to our physical well-being. For example, a review of studies found that depression increases the risk of coronary artery disease and ischaemic heart disease by between 50 and 100 per cent. Another study reported that chronic stress has a direct impact on the cardiovascular, nervous and immune systems, leading to increased susceptibility to a range of diseases. As a result of these associations, people with mental health problems are two to four times more likely to die prematurely, mostly from what one would regard as 'natural' causes such as cardiovascular disease.[8] This again raises the much-neglected fact that we are mind *and* body, not mind *or* body: the one constantly interacts with the other.

The dominant mental health issue in people with chronic pain is anxiety, notably anxiety that the pain indicates something serious, that this will occur, that it will be more than they can tolerate and that it might be life-threatening at some point. Second to anxiety is depression.

People who have long-term conditions, especially where pain is ongoing, and who are depressed, low in mood or anxious, are also less likely to adhere to their healthcare plans and requirements. Their eating and general self-care may deteriorate, which can exacerbate their current conditions as well as increase their chance of further illness or concerns such as infections, poor wound healing and stomach or bowel problems. They may become socially isolated or withdrawn, unable to become involved or disinterested in meaningful social relationships, hobbies and life activities. They may no longer be able to work or drive, and some may turn to substances or unhelpful activities to ease their boredom or distress.

What is central to so much of this is the spiralling deterioration in quality of life. A mixture of a long-term condition (even without chronic pain), isolation and a poor quality of life can lead to people taking their own lives.

Treating the pain

When you are living with chronic pain, it's likely that you will have visited your doctor on many occasions in order to try and control your symptoms and help you continue with everyday activities. You may have been referred to various specialists, each with a different opinion that has exacerbated your anxiety and stress, and which has in turn heightened your feeling of pain. Medication, or a cocktail of them, may have been prescribed, including some of the following:

- non-steroidal anti-inflammatory drugs (NSAIDs) (such as ibuprofen);
- paracetamol, which is known as a simple analgesic;
- weak opioids (such as codeine);
- strong opioids (such as morphine, tramadol or oxy-codone);
- epidural and spinal anaesthetic blocks;
- local nerve blocks (using local anaesthetics to target particular nerves);
- antidepressants, e.g. amitriptyline, a selective serotonin reuptake inhibitor (SSRI; such as citalopram, paroxetine or fluoxetine) or a serotonin–norepinephrine reuptake inhibitor (SNRI; such as venlafaxine or duloxetine;
- anticonvulsants (such as gabapentin);
- muscle relaxants (such as baclofen);
- tranquillizers (such as diazepam);
- corticosteroids (such as prednisone);
- topical medications (i.e. those applied to the skin, such as lidocaine patches or an anti-inflammatory gel).

These treatments may come with their own side effects that can be difficult to deal with, such as tiredness, change in appetite, constipation, loss of libido and poor concentration.

One concern of particular relevance is the crisis of opioid addiction and drug-related deaths that is occurring in the USA, to the extent that it is now being regarded as a public health issue demanding health and government intervention. A significant proportion of this crisis relates to the use of prescription painkiller medication rather than heroin street use.[9,10] Consequently, there is a widespread need for non-medicinal interventions to help people with chronic pain.

Non-medical treatments are often used in conjunction with medications, and they can be beneficial in different ways, even if only for short periods of time. They include formal and proven treatments such as physiotherapy, psychological therapy and mindfulness, as well as other interventions and strategies such as relaxation, pacing, heat therapy, exercise, eating plans that exclude certain foods and so forth. These additional interventions can be supportive and have positive psychological effects on the person even if they do not significantly alter the intensity of the pain.

Mindfulness is a non-medical treatment that has been actively researched over the years, especially more recently, due to its positive effect on managing pain and increasing an individual's perceived quality of life. Its effect on the stress response and functional brain activity will be discussed in detail further on.

Individual differences

We often say we are hurting when we experience pain. Depending on the level of severity, we may also feel discomfort, anguish or even agony as a result.

However, our threshold for experiencing and withstanding pain appears to vary considerably among individuals with different characteristics. For example, research has revealed a higher incidence of chronic pain and sensitivity to pain in women than men.[11] The biopsychosocial model of pain offers an explanation of how we experience pain differently. It suggests that biological factors (e.g. genetics), psychological factors (e.g. personality traits) and social factors (e.g. family and peer support) can all have a significant effect on pain experience.[12]

Mindfulness offers an opportunity to develop your self-capacity to manage your pain. Over time, it can give you a greater sense of control over your response to the physical sensations you experience, as well as your emotional reaction to these and the suffering that can come with pain. Two major studies[13,14] have found that mindfulness is more effective than opioid painkillers and that it shows significant positive results for those with chronic low back pain when compared with usual care (as did cognitive behavioural therapy). Importantly, the effects of mindfulness were still found at six months and 12 months compared with usual care and cognitive behavioural therapy.

Mindfulness practice: A Moment of Stillness

This exercise is a simple but effective way to begin to understand what mindfulness is about. It can be used as a starting point or as a marker of your progress as you become more involved in the process of mindfulness.

- Sit in stillness for two minutes.
- Pay attention to what thoughts and sensations are going through your mind. Is there an itch in your leg? Have you just remembered that you need to pay the phone bill? Do your shoulders feel tense? Is your heart pounding? Are you thinking about all the things on your to-do list?

What was it like sitting in stillness – did you feel comfortable, or were you in any physical or emotional discomfort? Did you start to feel calmer, or did your anxiety start to increase? Did the time go quickly or slowly? Why do you think that was?

3
Mindfulness and pain

A mindful approach

Mindfulness is about paying attention to, and accepting, your thoughts, feelings and responses in order to cultivate an alert and balanced state of mind.

- It is an approach to life that involves both practices and developing a way of being, a mindset.
- It can be developed and used by anyone, when appropriate.
- It is about encouraging your ability to be open to this moment of time for whatever it brings.
- It is not relaxation or an altered state of mind.
- It is a resource you can draw on in difficult times and a way to fully enjoy the good times.

A brief history of mindfulness

Mindfulness and meditation have become secularized from their original roots in Buddhism and other contemplative philosophies.[1] Meditations focusing on breathing and being present in the moment are an important part of Buddhist practices, and their effectiveness and usefulness have filtered through to the Western world over the centuries.

In 1979, colleagues at the University of Massachusetts developed a programme that integrated these mindfulness practices into a structured format to provide interventions for people with physical and emotional distress in a hospital setting. This programme became known as Mindfulness-Based Stress Reduction (MBSR), and it is now an internationally recognized approach that has been used worldwide for a variety of physical and emotional conditions.

Mindfulness practice: Breathe and Observe

- Breathe into your pain.
- Breathe into the centre of the pain.
- Breathe and release.
- Breathe and observe what is happening.
- Notice the tension in your body where the pain sits.
- Notice the tension in your body around the pain and beyond it.
- Simply observe it.
- Breathe and observe.
- How far does it extend?
- Where is it most painful?
- Breathe and observe what is happening.
- Breathe – observe – breathe – release – breathe.

Why mindfulness for pain?

Mindfulness and mindfulness meditations or practices bring with them some key factors. A central aspect of mindfulness is that everything in life is transient, it is impermanent. By developing and enhancing your focus, you become aware of how there are fluctuations in each moment of your existence. Your feelings and thoughts shift, your pain shifts, your situation shifts, and with each moment of life comes an altered perception. You notice the subtle nuances of change by observing and focusing.

Mindfulness enhances your focus, concentration and awareness, and by so doing it develops your ability to gather your energies to attend to a specific experience. This awareness and focused energy helps you to move towards your pain so that you can examine its location, intensity and variations, your response to it and how others respond to it. It opens up the possibility for you to respond to your pain not with fear and rejection, but with a kindness and sense of control.

Mindfulness develops your ability and capacity to both experience what is happening to you, including the good things as well as your pain, and to view it from above or from a step away. It gives you a 'meta-view' and perspective. 'Meta' means beyond, so this process involves thinking beyond your thoughts, feeling beyond your feelings and so forth. It is you having the experience and an awareness of the process of how you think, feel and respond to that experience. This does not imply dissociating or cutting off from an experience but rather viewing it from a distance.

Metacognition

The ability to think about one's thinking is what neuro-scientists call metacognition. It refers to the process of stepping back to see what you are doing, as an observer, watching and noticing your responses. Metacognition involves two distinct but interrelated areas – metacognitive knowledge and metacognitive regulation or control:

- Metacognitive knowledge involves awareness of your thinking, knowledge of yourself as a learner, and knowledge of the aspects of the task and strategies needed to carry it out.
- Metacognitive regulation involves your ability to manage your thinking processes, identify which strategies you actually use in order to make cognitive progress such as planning your approach to a task, evaluating its progress and, importantly, being able to change tactics or direction if there are difficulties.[2]

Metacognitive regulation is about developing awareness of what you think, do, feel and believe when you go through an experience. It's like seeing a rose as a whole flower but also being able to recognize that there are different parts of it (the petals, their colour variations, the stem, the stamen, the stalk, the leaves) that can be separate but that come together to form the flower. This awareness of the process of how these parts work separately and together does not make the rose any less of a flower or alter it in any way; it simply gives you a greater knowledge and perspective on it.

Mindfulness develops your capacity for, and draws on, metacognitive knowledge and metacognitive regulation. As the interest in mindfulness has grown significantly in recent years, an increasing number of research studies have investigated the potential benefits of mindfulness for pain. Below is a selection of some of the evidence gathered so far, and this will be discussed further in Chapter 7 on mindful awareness.

Mindfulness for pain

- Mindfulness reduces depression and the catastrophizing associated with pain. It also significantly improves outlook, acceptance and self-efficacy.[3]
- An online mindfulness-based cognitive therapy intervention is being found to be even more effective than psychoeducation for pain management.[4]
- The focused suggestion approach, which includes mindfulness meditation, is successfully used with both acute and chronic pain. This includes arthritis, post-injury pain from bone breaks, muscle tears and neuropathic pain.[5]

- Enhanced cognitive and emotional control are key effects of mindfulness meditation in relation to pain.[6,7]
- The activity of brain areas associated with the experience of pain is reduced through mindfulness meditation. Pain intensity is reported to be reduced by 40 per cent and pain unpleasantness by 57 per cent.[7] Mindfulness practitioners in a mindful state experience 29 per cent less anticipatory anxiety that they will feel pain.[8]
- Mindfulness has been shown to help patients experiencing pain-related anxiety and consequent reduction in their normal level of functioning.[9]

Mindfulness for chronic pain

- Mindfulness can reduce the phenomenon of 'anxiety sensitivity', or 'fear of anxiety', which is a phenomenon found to intensify the level of emotional distress related to the experience of chronic pain.[10]
- Immediate effects can be measured from a brief ten-minute mindfulness exercise used with people with chronic pain. These include reductions in pain-related distress and in interference of pain with social relations.[11]
- Greater levels of mindfulness are predictive of lower levels of disability, depression, anxiety and catastrophizing in chronic low back pain.[12]
- MBSR[13] is a useful intervention for people with failed back surgery syndrome pain.[14] It also leads to clinically relevant improvements in the level of pain disability and engagement in life activities for those with chronic

pain. MBSR can significantly improve pain intensity, pain-related distress, feelings of being in control of the pain and psychological well-being for those with chronic pain.[15–17]

- Patients with chronic pain show significant improvements in pain catastrophizing and mental health following a mindfulness-based chronic pain management course. Videoconferencing also seems to be an effective model of delivery for mindfulness.[18]

- Mindfulness-oriented recovery can target the downward spiral of chronic pain.[19]

- A review of 16 studies reported significantly lower pain intensity in chronic pain patients who underwent mindfulness-based interventions, and these reductions were generally well maintained.[20]

Mindfulness for acute pain

- Mindful attention reduces pain catastrophizing for acute experimental pain.[21]
- Mindfulness-based coping is better than distraction in acute experimental pain.[22]
- Experimentally induced pain leads to higher pain tolerance and lower distress when preceded by a short-term mindfulness intervention.[23]

Mindfulness for pain in specific conditions

- Around 85 per cent of people with persistent low back pain have been reported to be highly satisfied with a trial of mindfulness-based functional therapy. Improvements were found in physical functioning, pain catastrophizing and depression.[24]

- Mindfulness-based techniques bring greater accept-ance and quality of life in those experiencing chronic back pain.[25,26]

- An eight-week mindfulness meditation programme had positive effects for older adults with chronic low back pain, significantly improving pain acceptance and engagement with activities.[27]

- Mindfulness is showing lasting effects in terms of pain reduction with endometriosis.[28]

- Mindfulness training, which promotes non-reactive awareness – being aware of something without reacting to it in a knee-jerk manner – of sensory and emotional experiences, has therapeutic effects in IBS.

- Mindful awareness and acceptance treatment brings the broadest improvements in daily pain and stress reactivity for people with rheumatoid arthritis when compared with cognitive behavioural therapy and arthritis education.[29]

- The frequency of chronic migraines can be reduced by self-directed mindfulness training,[30] and MBSR can reduce the duration of migraines.[31] The frequency of chronic tension-type headache has been reported to be reduced after six sessions of mindfulness-based therapy.[32] Reduced pain interference and pain catastrophizing, as well as improved pain acceptance and self-efficacy, can result from mindfulness-based cognitive therapy.[33] Similarly, significant improvements in pain and quality of life in individuals with chronic headache have been shown through engagement with MBSR.[34]

Mindfulness for improving mental health in those experiencing pain

- A mindfulness intervention improved depression and trait anxiety in patients with chronic pain.[35]
- Mindfulness in Action therapy increases the ability of people in pain to manage their emotions and stress, and enjoy pleasant events.[36]

Mindfulness for pain in children and parents

- Acceptance and commitment therapy, containing principles of mindfulness, is effective as a treatment for improving parents' responses to their adolescent children experiencing chronic pain.[37]
- Mindful attention is successful in assisting children to focus their attention on experimental pain without increasing their pain intensity.[38]

Focused attention

Meditation, within the context of mindfulness, refers to paying attention to the present moment, for whatever it brings. By focusing on your breathing, the most automatic of functions, in this moment without evaluating or judging it, you are able to appreciate and absorb the moment for what it is – the sensations in your body, the sights, sounds and smells around you, the emotions you are experiencing – in a stable, balanced and non-reactive way. Instead of zoning out, mindfulness meditation brings your awareness to your life right now, grounding you and allowing you to be alive to this moment.

Mindfulness is about switching on, not switching off. This makes it different from relaxation as your intention is to bring your attention to each moment as it unfolds in life, even when some of those moments are distressing.

Mindfulness practice: Mindful Eating

- Take a piece of fruit, chocolate or any other food that is not too difficult to chew.
- Eat one piece as normal.
- Now take another piece of the food, place it on your tongue and let it sit there for a few moments.
- Bring all of your attention to the sensation in your mouth as you let the food remain in your mouth without chewing or swallowing it. What does it feel like in your mouth – rough or smooth? What does it taste like, and can you identify any elements to the taste that you had not noticed on the previous piece?
- Chew the food slowly. What other sensations do you feel? Is it difficult to resist the urge to swallow? Now swallow and notice the movements that come with this action.

4

My mind or my body

Chronic pain affects millions of people each year, but as only two-thirds make a full recovery,[1] it is necessary to find causes for why people have ongoing pain and what interventions might help.

Pain and the nervous system

The nervous system controls everything you do, including breathing, walking, thinking, feeling – and your pain. This system is made up of your brain, your spinal cord and all the nerves in your body. The brain is the control centre, and the spinal cord is the major highway to and from the brain. The body's nerves carry the messages to and from the spinal cord, and then up to the brain, so the brain can interpret them and take action.

The nerves are what give you pain signals. When you have chronic pain, your nerves can become so used to firing off these pain signals that things which should not be painful become very painful. For example, a small movement can very easily set off the pain signals in your nervous system because the nerves that send the pain signals are oversensitized and therefore easily triggered. This is referred to as central sensitization as it is caused by changes in the spinal cord and the brain.[2]

A good way to think of this is like an annoyingly sensitive smoke alarm. The smallest bit of smoke will set it off, and it doesn't seem logical that it should be set off so easily – sometimes we can't even see the smoke.

Pain and emotional memory

Pain is believed to have a memory, and certain things that you experience can trigger the memory of past painful experiences, which then come flooding back to you. You may or may not be consciously aware of the trigger until you make the link. This concept is central to symptoms such as flashbacks or intrusive thoughts in post-traumatic stress. The complexity of the brain means that it is capable of storing memories and sensations in our unconscious mind. These memories are not always clearly processed, which is what happens when people have experienced trauma of some kind.

The brain pathways that developed or were reinforced at the time of the trauma remain and are easily reactivated when something associated with the previous trauma happens, even if it is a similar smell, a touch or a simple behaviour. These triggers can remain from early infancy until death, and can emerge to a greater or lesser degree depending on how much of the experience has been processed. When a disruptive experience occurs, the normal processing of material is interfered with, so the input or stimulation does not go through the channels in the brain that would usually allow the experience to be analysed, interpreted, have thought and context given, and finally be put into memory.

With unexpected, traumatic or very distressing situations, the material associated with the experience is not sufficiently processed, particularly in the area known as the hippocampus, where it is interpreted and given meaning before being stored in memory. Consequently, this unprocessed or insufficiently processed material is easily activated, especially by triggers that remind the person consciously, but mostly unconsciously, of the past event. This trigger can throw the person into a flashback experience where the experience is relieved as though it were happening all over again. Alternatively, it can set off powerful thoughts about the event that are then difficult to put aside and can set the person on a downward spiral[3] and evoke physical pain.

Pain and no injury

Pain is often a result of an injury or is the body's way of warning you that something is wrong. People who have not had a specific injury or disease often cannot understand why they have pain, but in fact there are times where no explanation or medical reason can be found for why someone feels so much pain.

The invisible disease

Pain is invisible so it is often difficult to explain and pin-point. When you have an invisible problem, others may not understand it and their reactions may not be as kind or patient as you would like. You yourself may become angry or despondent and ask 'why me?' Chronic pain can be a great burden as it can affect so many areas of your life in such negative ways.

Conditions such as fibromyalgia and chronic fatigue are good examples of pain conditions that are difficult to diagnose and lead to people frequently feeling confused, frustrated and not believed.

The mind–body split

For centuries in the history of medicine, it was thought that the mind and body were two separate entities that had little influence on each other. However, in more recent years there has been a shift in recognizing the interconnectedness of the two and how one not only influences and affects the other, but can also directly alter its structure and process.

Professionals from whom you have sought advice and help may not have given this much consideration during your meetings: people with chronic pain are not usually asked about the emotions the pain is causing them or how it may be affecting their sexual life. Focusing on the physical aspect of pain alone means that only one component of your pain is being taken into account.[4]

The biopsychosocial model

The biopsychosocial model suggests that pain is influenced by the three components shown in Figure 4.1: a person's biology, psychology and social environment and relationships. All three may have equal or stronger influences at different times in an individual's life, but all interact on an ongoing basis.

This means that chronic pain can affect your life in a variety of ways and not just in the physical sense. Relationships may change; it might be difficult to

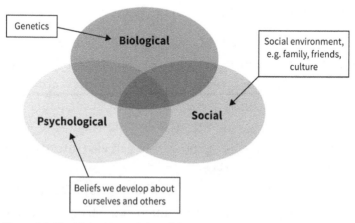

Figure 4.1 The biopsychosocial model

participate in activities you used to do; sex may be uncomfortable because of the pain; you may feel less attractive and confident in your own body; or your self-esteem and identity may have altered since living with chronic pain.

The psychodynamic approach

The psychodynamic approach, within the model put forward in this book, is an essential part of the 'psycho' part of the biopsychosocial model. It is based on the theory that your experiences from childhood into adult-hood considerably affect who you are in your adult years and how you act. The common theory is that if you are given regular, reliable and engaged care in your early years, you will grow to believe that you are lovable and valuable. On the other hand, if the care in your early years was unpredictable or lacking in boundaries, appropriate feedback or warmth, this can negatively influence how you view yourself as an adult.[4]

Biological, psychological, social and early life experi-ences are intricately linked, and who you are today is a result of all and every experience you have had up to this point – the wonderful, the boring and the horrible. You've learnt to survive in life and have many internal resources that work to your benefit. However, through life you may also have developed ways of protecting your-self, for example by not asking for help so you won't be disappointed if it isn't there, or thinking you'll be seen as a nuisance if you tell others you're in pain. These protective shields usually develop early in life, particularly through experiences with caregivers. The shields can, however, sometimes get in the way of managing your pain and also affect your relationships or quality of life.

Becoming more aware of, and alert to, these factors can help you gain a perspective on how you relate to yourself and others. It can help you to gain a clearer picture of what fits where, make sense of it and place it within a context[4]. Tables 4.1 and 4.2 are examples of charts you can draw up for yourself on a piece or paper or in a notebook to help you think about the different parts of the biopsychosocial model and how they interact with your own personal dynamics and impact on your current situation and life in general.

Table 4.1 Biological, psychological and social influences

Biological	Psychological	Social	Early experiences

Table 4.2 How these influences affect me

How they affect me	How they affect my relationships with professionals	How they affect my social and family relationships	How they impact on my pain and its management

Intensity control

The mind feels pain and also processes it. It sifts through the memories you have of pain experiences in the past in order to find a solution to your current pain. Although this is in the first instance done as a way of remedying your current pain, what it inadvertently does is activate your old memories. However, if your pain is chronic, a solution isn't found and you are left with re-evoked thoughts, emotions and memories of past pain. This can lead to feelings of distress, fear, anger or hopelessness, which in turn increase your levels of stress and lead to a decline in your physical and emotional health, a decrease in efficiency of your immune system and healing process, and a decrease in your quality of life.

This activation of previous memories controls both the intensity and duration of the pain. As previously mentioned, your brain, through repeated cycles of pain, becomes more attuned and sensitive to pain, with an increased number of neuronal pathways that light up and activate whenever there is any pain or anticipation of pain.[2]

By starting to engage more with your thoughts, and by understanding the events that have brought you to where you are now, feelings and memories may be brought to the fore that may be painful or upsetting. Should this happen, be aware of the sensation but manage it in a positive way, by listening to music or talking to a friend, for example. If the feelings are very distressing, you should seek the input of a qualified professional. Therapy should not be regarded as embarrassing or intimidating; it is simply two people coming together to consider your life and develop your understanding of these feelings to better deal with them.

Mindfulness practice: A Moment of Calm in Two Minutes

This two-minute breathing exercise is an excellent introduction to how focusing on your breathing can help to settle and ground you. It is particularly useful when your chest or stomach feels tight, your heart is pounding or you are feeling bombarded by distressing thoughts. It can be done at any time and in any place when you feel off-balance or anxious – before giving a presentation or taking an exam, after a difficult conversation, in the staff room at work, or when pain strikes.

- Sit in a chair with your eyes open or closed and place one hand on your stomach, feeling it rise and fall. Without forcing your breath in any way, silently count 'in, 2, 3, 4' on the inbreath and 'out, 2, 3, 4' on the outbreath. Repeat this three times.

- Breathe in for the same amount of time as above, but count only 'in, 2, 3' on the inbreath and 'out, 2, 3' on the outbreath. Repeat this three times and then reduce it to 'in, 2, out, 2' and repeat three times. Now take one breath in and one breath out, without counting. If this feels difficult, think 'in' and 'out' to the rhythm of your breathing. Repeat three times.

- Take a moment to think about how you feel. Do you feel calmer? Is your breathing more regular? Do you feel less tense, and have your physical symptoms of anxiety subsided a little?

- Take this moment of calm with you, knowing that returning to a calmer and more balanced state of mind can be as simple as breathing.

When you take the time to sit in stillness, your mind often starts to fill with thoughts, ruminations, anxieties and fears related to your pain. In the following sections, the mindfulness practices will help to develop your focus, allowing you to take a step back from these worries.

Minds wander because that's what minds do.

5

Stress and pain

Stress is a biological and psychological response experienced on encountering a threat, whether that threat be real or thought to be real. Your body's response to stress is a primitive, automatic mechanism to ensure your survival. It is activated at the smallest hint of danger and is always on alert for any threatening situation.

Your brain cannot distinguish between the different types of stressful or distressing situations that occur in life. It doesn't know that the tension you feel when in pain is different from the stress you feel from being in a potentially life-threatening situation. It interprets both as one and the same thing, in that it thinks you are in danger even if you are not. Your being in pain and reacting to it is perceived as a potential threat to your survival – referred to as a perceived threat because you are not actually in true danger as you would be if a tiger jumped out at you.

Your brain, however, kicks into gear at any actual or perceived signal of danger. Threat sets off a physiological

Table 5.1 Sympathetic and parasympathetic systems

Sympathetic system – go mode	Parasympathetic system – rest mode
Adrenaline and cortisol released into the blood Breathing rate increases Heart rate rises Energy is directed to the heart, muscles and breathing Digestive process shuts down	Noradrenaline released into blood Breathing rate decreases Heart rate falls Energy is redirected to other organs in body that help with digestion, absorption, excretion and other essential functions

reaction via a branch of the nervous system called the sympathetic nervous system, which switches you into 'go' mode (see Table 5.1). Once the threatening situation has passed, your body should return to its normal state. It does this in response to activation of another part of the system, the parasympathetic system, which puts you back into 'rest' mode (see Figure 5.1).

However, when stress, which starts in your head and activates your body's physiological response, is interpreted

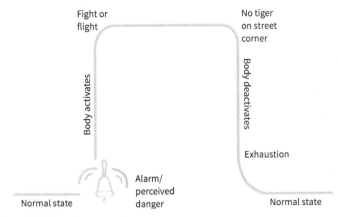

Figure 5.1 The stress response

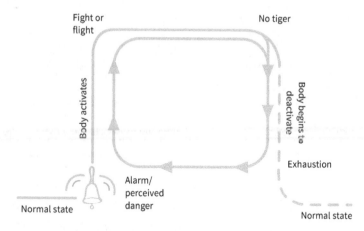

Figure 5.2 The chronic/ongoing stress response

by your brain as perceived danger and is continually experienced, your sympathetic nervous system remains in a more active state than it needs to be. This phenomenon is extremely important because, over time, it can bring about both physical and psychological problems as your mind and body become exhausted (see Figure 5.2).

What non-stop stress can cause

There is known to be a link between stress and multiple conditions, such as:

- damage to organs and memory cells
- fatty deposits around the waist
- ageing
- hypertension

- heart disease
- diabetes
- pain conditions
- infertility
- loss of libido
- worse work performance
- distorted thinking
- IBS
- depression
- anxiety and panic attacks
- rheumatoid arthritis
- cancer
- sleep
- impotence
- relationship difficulties
- decrease in quality of life.

In terms of pain, your body judges a situation and decides whether or not it is stressful. This decision is made based on sensory input and processing (i.e. the things you see and hear in the situation) and also on stored memories (i.e. what happened the last time you were in a similar situation). Pain can be triggered by a stressful situation or can exacerbate it. However, being in pain can certainly lead to stress, so a vicious cycle is step up (see Figure 5.3 overleaf).

Although this vicious cycle is not uncommon, it can make everyday life more difficult. The activity of the stress response, with its physiological reactions, can lead

Figure 5.3 The pain–stress cycle

to greater muscle tension and exhaustion, which can then make the pain more intense. If you consider that one of the responses when your brain perceives danger (stress) is to release chemicals to help you fight off the tiger or run with determination, and later to return your body to a normal state, you can see how pain will produce an extra dose of hormones. These will at first put you on high alert, but afterwards wear off, potentially leaving you feeling tired and even depressed. Each time you are in pain, your body will react in this way. Mindful breathing can, however, help to reduce the impact of the stress response.

Paying attention

Part of mindfulness is taking the time to pay attention to yourself and to your body. This may be difficult because of the sensations of pain, but it can be started slowly and in small stages. The Body Focus practice encourages you to recognize where the primary pain or sensation is occurring, its location, quality and intensity, and also which other parts of your body may be affected as an extension of the primary source of pain. In addition to this, you will start to realize that there are parts of your body, even if only a hand or a finger, that are not in pain or are in less pain.

In a positive way, this practice helps you to reconnect to your body, as when we are in pain we lose faith in our bodies. This practice reminds you that there are various parts that make up your physical existence in the world, and they all require attention and care. This is important because chronic pain can distort your beliefs about yourself as well as your body.

Mindfulness practice: Body Focus

Find a quiet place to carry out this practice. Switch your phone to silent or leave it in another room, and ask others around you not to disturb you unless it is an emergency. Ensure you are wearing comfortable clothing and that you will be warm enough; perhaps have a blanket nearby, as your body temperature will drop. This is also an excellent practice for physical pain.

- Choose a position that is comfortable and works well for you. The ideal position is lying flat on your back on the floor (see Figure 5.4), on a rug or blanket if there is no carpet, with a cushion for your head if this increases your comfort.

- Use any cushions, blankets or other supports that will help you to feel comfortable.

- If it's more comfortable, place your legs, either straight or bent, up on a chair (see Figure 5.5). An alternative is lying on a bed, especially if you have difficulty getting down to the floor. If you find lying down uncomfortable or difficult, you can sit in a chair that provides sufficient support (see Figure 5.6), using footstools or cushions to ensure your comfort. If sitting is not ideal, you can stand or lean against a wall to make sure you have a steady object to lean on (see Figure 5.7).

Figure 5.4 Lying on the floor

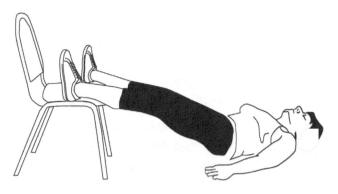

Figure 5.5 Lying on the floor with feet up on a chair

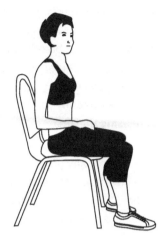

Figure 5.6 Sitting in a chair

Figure 5.7 Standing against a wall

- A note about breathing. When the track says 'breathe into your toes' or any other part of your body, it is meant metaphorically. Physiologically, we are unable to breathe into any part of our body other than our lungs, so this is about imagining the breath moving through your body. By placing your breath into an area of your body in your imagination, you are bringing attention and focus to it and relaxing the area.

- Before starting the practice, take a moment to think about how you are feeling. Take note of any physical sensations of stress or anxiety, as well as any thoughts or emotions that are at the forefront of your mind. Tell yourself that this is very important for your psychological and physical well-being.

🔊 Listen to the Body Focus practice, which you will find in the audio file accompanying this book. A written sample of the wording of the practice can be found below. It has been included so that you can get an idea of what it is about and be reassured that there is nothing in any of the practices that aim to put you into a trance-like or altered state of mind. All you are doing is breathing.

After the practice, take a few moments to think about your response to it before moving. Did you give yourself the time and space to do the practice? What were your expectations before the practice, and were they reasonable? For example, did you expect to feel much calmer but now feel frustrated because you still feel stressed? Were you cynical at first, but found the practice enjoyable and relaxing?

Most people fall asleep when they first do this practice. However, if you find that you continually fall asleep when doing it, it is helpful to do it sitting up until you are able to remain alert throughout. The purpose of the practice is to bring awareness to your body, not send you off to sleep.

Sample transcript from the Body Focus practice

The intention is to bring awareness to the different parts of the body without moving or stretching them in any way. It is about experiencing the sensations within your body, making no demands on it.

As you breathe in and out, become aware that this is your body, all of it, for whatever it is: the parts that work well and keep you alive, and the parts that are damaged and in pain.

Now focus on the big toe of your left foot. Become aware of the existence of this part of your body and the sensations that might be there. Let your attention go deep into the toe, not moving it, just observing it and feeling whatever is or isn't happening in it at this moment. If you feel no sensations, that too is fine. Simply acknowledge whatever is there.

Now move your focus to the little toe on the left foot – and to all the toes. Become aware of the feelings within the toes, acknowledge them, and breathe deep into the toes on an inbreath. And on an outbreath, let go of your awareness of the toes, letting their existence drift and dissolve from your mind.

Now bring your attention to the sole of your left foot, focusing on any sensations deep within the foot, aware of the air against it, your instep, the heel against the floor. Breathing in and out of it, and on the outbreath let go of your awareness of it and bring it to the top of the left foot, becoming familiar with the sensations in this part of your body, of all the small bones that make up the foot. Breathing all the way into it, and then on an outbreath letting it dissolve from awareness.

Moving your focus to the left ankle, feeling and acknowledging whatever it is that is there, aware of the bones that come together to form a joint. Breathing into it and out of it, letting it go. Now focus on the foot and ankle as a whole, breathing deep into it. Let your breath travel, in your mind's eye, all the way down from the nostrils, through the chest and abdomen, down the left leg and into the foot and ankle, aware of the oxygen coming to it; and when it gets there, release and let the breath travel all the way back out through the nostrils, and on an outbreath let the foot and ankle dissolve from your awareness.

Remember, the practices are there to help you to switch on, not to switch off.

6

Pain and movement

A common issue when people are in pain is that their physical activity is reduced. Either they cannot exercise or they become reluctant to engage because they are in pain or they fear the pain will worsen with exercise.

In the past, people were told to rest if, for example, they had backache. Now, however, the exact opposite has been found to be of particular importance. For those who have chronic pain, fear and anxiety can prevent them from meeting with friends or partaking in social activities that they once enjoyed. This is common and understandable – you may be in too much pain to socialize, too tired, unable to concentrate or perhaps anxious that further injury or pain may occur.

However, movement keeps your muscles and joints in better health and prevents the effects of further disruption caused by inactivity, such as poor circulation, muscle waste and stiffness. The effects are not only physical but psychological too, as being cooped up and immobile can lead to isolation, depression and fear (see Figure 6.1 overleaf).

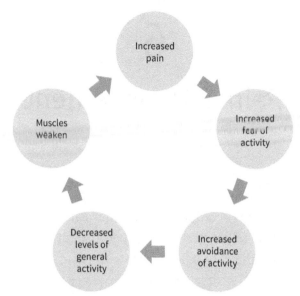

Figure 6.1 The pain–activity cycle

Being more aware of what is happening through mindfulness will help you to intervene at any point in the cycle and manage your anxieties.

It is essential that you get moving. The only time you should not is if you have specifically been advised not to. People who do regular activity have:[1]

- up to a 35 per cent lower risk of coronary heart disease and stroke;
- up to a 50 per cent lower risk of type 2 diabetes;
- up to a 50 per cent lower risk of colon cancer;
- up to a 2 per cent lower risk of breast cancer;
- a 30 per cent lower risk of early death;

- up to an 83 per cent lower risk of osteoarthritis;
- up to a 68 per cent lower risk of hip fracture;
- a 30 per cent lower risk of falls among older adults;
- up to a 30 per cent lower risk of depression;
- up to a 30 per cent lower risk of dementia.

There are many things you can do, even if you're chair-bound.

Mindful body movement

The movements described are gentle, stretching ones to increase and maintain mobility. However, even these moves may not be possible if you are severely ill, in a wheelchair, bed-ridden, in too much pain or too frail. Should this be the case, other exercises can be implemented. The point is that whatever you do, no matter how small, it can be done in a way that integrates the movement with your breathing in a mindful and caring way.

These movements are only suggestions and are not a substitute for continuing with any other intervention you have been recommended by a relevant healthcare professional. They can also ease you into gentle activity if you have tended to shy away from it in the past.

- It cannot be emphasized enough that you should only attempt what you can.
- If you have any physical difficulties, make sure there is someone nearby who can assist you if needed.

- Stand on a non-slip surface in bare feet or in non-slip shoes.
- If you have to stand on a slippery surface, make sure you aren't wearing heels or don't have socks on.

Why not do the moves with someone else? One person can talk it through while the other does the movements, before switching around. That way, you both get to do the exercises and can also be of help to each other.

Many of the exercises can be done sitting in a chair – a chair without arms such as a dining room chair – if necessary.

Standing movements (or movements on a chair)

If you are standing, have your feet hip width apart so you can balance yourself. Keep your knees soft and your hips loose, imagining there is a small weight attached to your tailbone. Tuck your navel in towards your spine as though you are pulling in your stomach to tighten your belt. Relax your shoulders into your back, lightly tuck in your chin, and let your head balance on top of your spine. Breathe in, and on an outbreath let unwanted tension be released. On an inbreath, take in a feeling of relaxed strength. This is referred to as the neutral position.

Be aware of each movement and let your breath flow in and out, without forcing it or breathing too deeply.

Shoulder shrugs

These can be done sitting on a chair or standing. If you are standing in the neutral position, let your arms hang loosely by your sides. Breathe out and lift your shoulders up towards your ears. Hold them there, breathe in, and as you breathe out relax your shoulders down into your back. Repeat this four times.

Shoulder circles forwards

The next move involves shoulder circles in a *forward* direction. From a neutral point, bring your right shoulder up to your ear, rotate the shoulder forwards, down, around to the back, and then towards the ear, and continue with three more circles.

Repeat this move four times with the left shoulder, returning to the neutral position at the end.

Shoulder circles backwards

Now do *backward* shoulder circles. From the neutral position, lift your right shoulder up to your right ear, then rotate it back towards your shoulder blade, down towards the floor, forwards and then up to the ear. Continue with three more circles, relaxing your shoulder at the end.

Now change to the left shoulder and repeat this four times, returning to the neutral position at the end.

Chest stretch

The first section of this exercise can be done standing or alternatively sitting on a chair. Check your posture so that

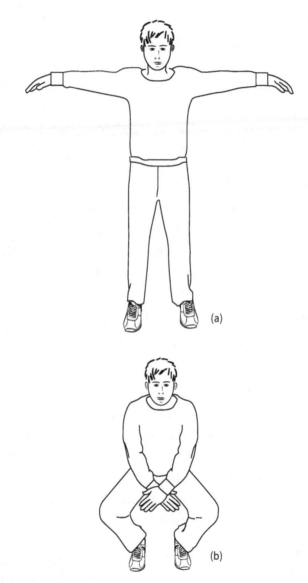

(a)

(b)

Figure 6.2(a) and (b) Chest stretch

your feet are hip width apart, your shoulders are relaxed and your head is gently balanced. Let your arms hang at your sides.

This move is like a bird spreading its wings out to the side and then bringing them in again. So, with your arms down, cross your hands in front of you. From this position, inhale while you extend both arms to shoulder height, arms parallel to the floor, and on an outbreath, bring the arms back down so that your hands cross over each other. Repeat this three times in a flowing movement.

Now, after spreading your arms out as described above, gently bend the knees at the same time as you bring your arms down to cross your hands (see Figure 6.2). Then, as you lift your arms up again, straighten your knees. Repeat this three times at an easy pace and then relax your knees and arms.

Neck and shoulder tension release

This can be done sitting or standing. Have relaxed but strong shoulders, i.e. don't slouch or stick your chin out as you may hurt your neck. Gently tilt your head forwards so that your chin moves towards your chest, and then lift it to the neutral position. Don't tilt your head back. Slowly drop your chin and raise it, and gently drop it and raise it, and finally lower your chin and come back to the centre.

Now, with relaxed but erect shoulders, gently turn your head to the left, bring it back to towards the centre and then turn it to the right in one flowing movement. Without forcing it, repeat this three times and then bring your head back to the centre.

From a central position of your head, gently tilt your left ear towards your left shoulder, keeping the ear in line with the shoulder so that your head is not tilting forwards. Keep your shoulders relaxed. Only go as far as is comfortable and breathe into the position (count to 8). Then return to the centre. Now tilt your right ear towards your right shoulder, keeping a straight line and not forcing the movement (again count to 8). Return to the central position and repeat, and finally return to the centre.

Now breathe out and slowly drop your head to your chest, releasing any tension. Breathe in, and as you breathe out, raise your head back to the neutral position. Repeat this three times.

Full arm circles

The following movement is a full arm circle and can be done sitting or standing. Be careful not to breathe too deeply, but rather allow the flow of breath to go with the movements.

Standing in your neutral position, or sitting, bring your hands to cross in front of you. Breathe in as you start to circle the arms around, with the arms crossing as though you are removing a jumper or T-shirt, and continue with the circle (see Figure 6.3), breathing out as your arms come down. Breathe in and continue the circle upwards,

Figure 6.3 Full arm circles

and then breathe out as your arms come down. Repeat twice more, and then relax your arms by your sides.

Arm lifts

The focus will now be on lifting the arms. Standing upright, or sitting, breathe out and lift the right arm up in front of you all the way until the back of your hand is up towards the ceiling, keeping your elbow soft and your arm rounded. Breathe in and bring the arm down towards your side. Repeat this three more times. Relax the arm, change to the left arm and do the same movements.

Arm lifts alternating

This can be done sitting or standing. Both arms will now be used, but you will alternate them. Keeping the same posture as before, check that your hips are facing straight ahead if you are standing, and that your weight is evenly spread. Place your arms by your sides, and then lift your left arm towards the ceiling; as you bring it down, lift your right arm up towards the ceiling, so that the arms cross over, with the one arm following the other. Repeat this three more times, but after the fourth time keep both arms raised above your head.

Upward stretch

Lift your left arm towards the sky, pointing your fingers upwards. Breathe into the stretch, keeping your feet flat on the ground and your shoulder relaxed. Reach up straight.

Relax the left shoulder a little and switch to the right arm, stretching the fingers towards the sky, reaching up as though trying to pick a cloud out of the sky, without tilting or overstretching. Now relax the right shoulder and stretch again with the left one, breathing into the stretch; then relax that shoulder and stretch with the right arm, breathing into the stretch. On an outbreath, bring both your arms down to your sides, becoming aware of the changes in sensation in your hands, arms and torso.

Side bends

The next movement involves gently bending sideways and can be done sitting or standing. If you are standing, relax your shoulders into your back, with your hips facing forwards, your feet apart and your knees soft. With your arms relaxed by your sides, breathe in and on the outbreath gently run your right arm down the side of your right thigh so that you are bending your body from the waist and allowing the left side of your body to be stretched (see Figure 6.4(a) overleaf). If you are doing the exercise in a sitting position, make sure your arm is straight and move your fingers towards the floor. Only go as far as you can with this movement. Watch that your body is in a straight line and that you are not leaning forward or twisting your shoulders.

Breathe in, and on the outbreath come back to the upright position using the muscles in the core of your body to lift your body and not just your shoulder. Check your posture, and on an outbreath bend to your left three more times, remembering to breathe and to bend from the waist in a straight line. Return to the centre.

Repeat the same movement four times on the left side (see Figure 6.4(b) overleaf), remembering to breathe, and then return to the centre using your core muscles and bending and straightening up from the waist. Notice the areas of tension and when you tend to stop breathing. At the end, return to the centre position.

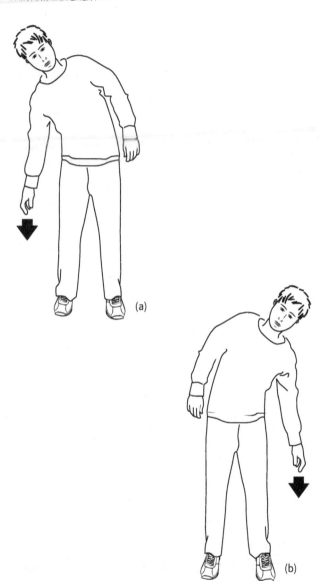

Figure 6.4(a) and (b) Side bends

Floor movements

Now place yourself on the floor, if you can, as the following moves will be done lying on a mat or soft carpet.

Foot circles, foot flexes and one-leg circles

Lie on your back with your knees bent. Roll your hips slightly to ensure that they are evenly placed on the mat or carpet. Check that your spine is keeping its natural C-shaped curve in the small of the back. This is the relaxation position.

Bend your left leg towards your chest and clasp your hands behind your left knee – not on the knee but on the back of the thigh just below the knee – so that your calf is parallel to the floor.

Figure 6.5 Foot circles

Gently circle the left foot clockwise four times (see Figure 6.5 on the previous page), keeping the movement continuous. Now circle it anticlockwise four times.

Check that the upper part of your body is relaxed. Still holding your thigh, point the toes of the left foot towards your chin and then in the opposite direction, away from you, repeating this four times. Remember to breathe naturally. Now hug your left knee closer to your chest, releasing the tension, and return the foot to the floor.

Now repeat the whole set of moves with the opposite foot, i.e. using the right leg. Check that the upper part of your body is relaxed. Still holding your thigh, point the toes of the right foot towards your chin and then in the opposite direction, away from you. Again, repeat this four times, remembering to breathe naturally. Now hug your right knee closer to your chest, releasing the tension, and return the foot to the floor.

Extend both your legs out so that you are lying straight on the floor for the next exercise.

Pelvic tilt

We will now get the pelvis and lower back moving. So, lying on the floor, knees bent, feet hip width apart, and the spine in its C-shaped curve, check that your hips are even and that you are not putting more pressure on one side than on the other. Relax your upper body.

Breathe in, engage your pelvic floor muscles, and pull your navel towards your spine. As you breathe out, start to press your waist into the floor so that your pelvic area begins to rise slightly, curling the pelvis inwards (see Figure 6.6(a)). Keep your hips on the floor and hold this position. Breathe in, breathe out, breathe in and on the next outbreath slowly roll the pelvis back to its neutral position (see Figure 6.6(b)).

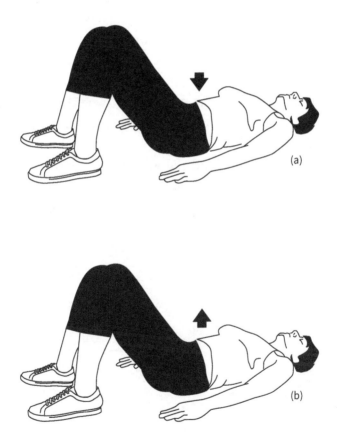

Figure 6.6(a) and (b) Pelvic tilt

Ending off

Roll on to your side (see Figure 6.7). Carefully and gradually bring yourself up from the floor, pausing for a moment before standing up. There is no rush, and you should be cautious not to force or jar your body.

A complete set of movements can be found on the CDs of guided meditations accompanying the book *Life Happens* (<http://www.lifehappens-mindfulness.com/books/life-happens/>, also available as an mp3 download).

Try one or two moves and become familiar with them before moving on to the next one or two. This will help you to know which ones are manageable and which are too painful or difficult.

You don't need attend the gym or run around a field in order to keep fit. The gentle moves provided in this chapter can help to introduce you to greater body fitness or to restart it. They can also be used in conjunction with other exercises or even adapted to suit your situation. Whatever the case, taking care when exercising,

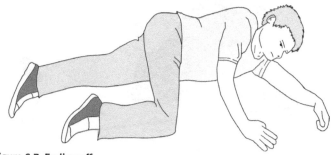

Figure 6.7 Ending off

and remember that breathing correctly when doing so is important for our health and safety.

A walk with a difference

The following is a formal mindful movement practice that is easy to do if you are able to walk.

Mindfulness practice: Let's Go for a Walk

This practice is an example of an activity that you may do frequently without paying any attention to what you are doing. It has been adapted from the traditional walking meditation to include a broader perspective. Focusing your attention on to your automatic functions can ground and balance you, and this walking practice can be used when anxieties and stresses seem to be getting on top of you. Try it as a short break from work, studying or activities, or when you can feel your frustrations growing.

- Take a walk in the garden, a park or wherever is convenient. Keeping your eyes lowered, bring your attention to the physical sensations of walking. Feel the changes in pressure as you place your feet on the ground, be aware of your breathing; pay attention to the rhythm of your footsteps and the slight swinging motion of your arms. Acknowledge any emotions or sensations that come into your mind.

- Lift your eyes to the world around you. Little by little, pay special attention to the sights, sounds and smells of your environment. Take everything in: the movement, the stillness, the light, the shade, the chaos and the peace. Allow yourself to be open to your environment and its effect on you.

- Shift your focus to your connection to the outside world and the impact you are having on your environment. Let your breathing flow naturally, becoming part of the world around you. Feel the stability of the ground beneath your feet and let it strengthen you. Notice any changes in the sensations and feelings you are experiencing, and acknowledge that the world around you is having an impact on you, just as you have an influence on the environment.

- Finally, take a mental step back from such an active involvement in the sensations of the environment. Continue to observe your breathing gently as a space forms between you and the outside world. You are aware of your surroundings, sensitive to them and appreciative of them, but the sensations arising from them are not the entirety of your experience. Take a moment to appreciate this moment, knowing you can take this sense of peace and clarity with you when you step back into your everyday activities.

7

Mindful awareness – mindful breathing

Breathing and focusing

Breathing is essential for survival, but it also plays a key role in the management of stress. If you watch someone sleeping, you will notice how the chest rises and falls in a rhythmic way and breathing comes easily and naturally in a deep, smooth and calming rhythm.

But although everyone instinctively knows how to breathe, we do not necessarily know how to breathe well. We have a tendency to breathe into the shallowest part of our lungs – around the shoulders and upper chest area – which have the least flexibility and space. Think of what happens when people are told to take a deep breath – they usually lift their shoulders rather than expand the area above their navel, which is where there is the most room for expansion of the lungs. So we tend to have a reduced amount of air entering our lungs, and the pattern of our breathing is shallow and irregular. Consequently, we may not be breathing as effectively as we could, and this can be particularly so when our bodies are tense from pain or fear of pain.

Paying attention to your breathing and focusing on it during the practices, and at other times, will increase the levels of oxygen entering your bloodstream and your brain. This can intercept the stress response before it has damaging effects from unnecessary activation[1] and can promote your own sense of well-being. In addition, mindfulness may help to regulate the release of neuro-transmitters and increase the number of connections between different areas of the brain.[1] These physical changes in the brain lead to improved function, which can influence your emotional state.

Brain imaging technologies have enabled psychologists and neuroscientists to study the effects of mindfulness in new and advanced ways. Functional magnetic resonance imaging (fMRI) scans are able to give visual indications of changes in brain structure before and after adopting mindfulness practices, as well as compare the brains of people who practise mindfulness and those who don't. The research shows that mindfulness meditation can:

- increase the brain's grey matter in areas responsible for regulating emotions, sensations and thoughts;[2]
- increase impulse control[3] and improve reasoning and decision-making skills;[4]
- improve executive functions such as memory and attention;[5]

- decrease stress and levels of stress hormones, improve quality of life, improve mood, decrease levels of depression and reduce the effects of trauma;[6]
- improve quality of sleep, promote a sense of happiness and improve relationship satisfaction.[7]

Mindfulness meditation impacts measurable brain circuits more than relaxation does. Inflammation, especially chronic inflammation in which the body's immune system's defence response is overactive even if there is no infection or injury, is central to many health problems such as cancer, heart disease, diabetes, stroke and Alzheimer's disease. Mindfulness reduces some of this inflammation by bringing about changes in the brain's functional connectivity. It also helps the brain to manage stress, which is a known trigger of inflammation, as well as increase the function of the immune system.[8]

Conversely, stress and the stress hormone cortisol disrupt grey and white matter connectivity.[9] Chronic pain leads to structural changes in the brain, such as changes in volume of the brain's outer layer of grey matter, which is where large numbers of neurons involved with storing and processing information tend to accumulate. Stress also interferes with connectivity within the underlying white matter, which contains communication or communication networks between various brain regions. In short, chronic stress and chronic pain compromise the cells that store and process information as well as the network fibres that allow the information to be passed between areas of the brain.

As described above, mindfulness has been shown to increase the volume of grey matter in areas associated with emotional regulation, understanding and putting words to experiences, thinking and planning, among others. It deactivates the brain's default mode, which generates spontaneous wandering thoughts (thoughts that are not necessarily being controlled or screened in a good way), contributes to the maintenance of your beliefs about yourself or sense of self, and is associated with anxiety and depression. It also allows for better connections between the default network mode and the executive network mode, which facilitates good planning, organizing and so forth. By increasing the connectivity between these two opposing networks, it encourages greater balance between them.[8]

Mindfulness also allows you to build your internal resilience and resourcefulness. You will gain more awareness of why you respond as you do and how you can have control over your reactions and the responses to what you feel, think and do, and the choices that you make. However, these benefits cannot happen if you do not do the practices. It is through the ongoing focusing and refocusing that your brain makes connections. What fires together, wires together – which mean that when you do the practices, the neurons in your brain that are activated can develop new positive pathways, and by creating these, the old negative, harsh ones that tend to look for the negative aspects are softened and weakened.

We all possess what is referred to as a negative bias. This is our mind's alertness to picking up any signs of unhelpful, dangerous or unpleasant stimuli or prods so that they can be evaluated quickly in order to ensure our survival. This bias can become overdeveloped when life situations or experiences are difficult, and far outweigh what is positive. Mindfulness helps to balance this bias by encouraging you to create a space in which you can decide how helpful or unhelpful a stimulus is before reacting to it.

It has been found that mindfulness works better than a placebo in reducing pain. The mechanisms in the brain that it uses to reduce the pain are different from those that would normally stimulate your body's pain-blocking process of producing natural opioids.[10] This is an important finding as it opens up a new way for people to use as a pain management intervention rather than solely relying on medication.

Mindful awareness

Mindful awareness and mindful breathing can be seen as the same thing as they both pay close attention to your breathing, so the terms are used interchangeably in this book.

Meditation or sitting positions

The meditation positions, or sitting positions as they are often called, were illustrated as examples under the Body Focus section. You may find it more comfortable sitting upright on your bed or floor. Whenever you are sitting for any period of time, even when you are sitting in a chair, it is important to make sure that your hips are positioned higher than your knees. There is no need for you to suffer, so use props, cushions, blankets or anything else to help you feel comfortable. However, when you are sitting, always be aware of your back being upright, your chest and heart open and your head gently balanced on your neck.

If you cannot sit, lie on the floor, ensuring that your neck and back are well supported. If you need to stand for the practice, it is essential that you lean against a wall or hold on to a chair to prevent falling.

There should be a softness and openness to your approach to all the practices. Bring to them a sense of kindness and curiosity. They can be done sitting at an office desk or on a bench in the garden. There will always be noise around you, but try to find a place where you will not be interrupted and ensure that your phone is turned off.

Right or wrong way

There is no right or wrong way, no set goal or score sheet when doing these practices. Your mind will inevitably drift when you are meditating, your thoughts will intrude, and your concentration will rapidly flit about. This will happen both at first and even after many years of practice. The aim, however, is not to empty your mind but to become aware of what is happening within it and with it: your thoughts, emotions and urges. Acknowledge what is there without reacting, simply saying *thought* when a thought comes up or *feeling* when a feeling emerges. It's about recognizing the activity for what it is (e.g. thinking) and then letting it be there without attending to it.

Whenever your mind drifts or gets into a story, acknowledge it, step away from it and bring your attention back to your breathing – focus and refocus no matter how often this happens. It will happen over and over again because that's what minds do – they think, connect, make links, activate emotions and impulses and react. Your mind is simply doing its job, but your job is to focus its energy and train it to refocus that energy, either on your breathing or, at other times in your life, on a situation or experience. The main point is that you keep doing the practices as each time you do, you are developing the structures in your brain, your emotional resilience and your own internal sense of stability and belief.

The following practice is one that you will come to rely on for years to come. It is one of the key meditations that is central to mindfulness practice, and its benefits are far-reaching. It is truly worth doing on a regular basis.

Mindfulness practice: Mindful Awareness

Mindful awareness is about becoming aware of what is happening within yourself, which encourages you to bring your focus and attention to your internal experiences and how they shift.

🔊 There are two options for this practice on the audio download: a 20-minute and a five-minute version. Begin with the five-minute version, and once this feels familiar move on to the 20-minute one if you can. Ideally, do the 20-minute version a few times per week, and the five-minute one on the other days.

Below you will see a transcript of the five-minute mindful awareness breathing practice. It has been included to show you that there is nothing strange or peculiar about the practices. You are breathing anyway, so these practices help you to focus your breathing and to use it in a remarkably helpful way.

You'll notice that each guided meditation has a 'bong' sound at the beginning and the end to help prepare you.

Sample transcript from the Mindful Awareness practice (five-minute version)

With your eyes closed, being alert and awake, bring your attention to your breathing, and to the movement of the breath as it comes in and out of your body. Simply observe your breathing – watching the path it takes as it travels in at the nose, down to the abdomen and then out again though the nose.

Staying focused on the breath, without forcing it in any way. Being here, with each inbreath and with each outbreath, letting one follow on from the other.

Use your breath as an anchor. Allow the breath to anchor you to the centre within your abdomen, that part that is stable, focused and present. Follow the breath to your anchor, bringing with it a new beginning . . . and with each outbreath a letting-go.

Be aware of each breath nourishing and grounding you, renewing and letting go, one breath following the other. Allow it to bring with it a stillness and a feeling of balance, grounding you right here, right now. Letting it anchor you, gently and kindly, to this moment, and to this moment.

As the intensity begins to ease, let your attention spread to include all of your body, and engage your breath in a rhythmic flow that moves in and out of your body as a whole.

Gradually let your awareness begin to take in the sounds around you and within you, simply letting them exist in harmony with you, as you breathe. Sitting in stillness, in this moment.

Feeling grounded, feeling balanced. Gently allow all of your senses to be awake, to be alert and alive to all that is happening within you and around you. Acknowledge with kindness that you spent this time living each moment of your life, with whatever came with it, in a mindful, balanced and open way, and that you now have the choice of how you wish to live this moment of your life, and this moment.

When you notice that difficult thoughts are entering your mind or consciousness, acknowledge them, know that they are there, but do not engage with them. Let them drift past, let them enter and exit your mind as you continue to breathe.

Consider your thoughts as clouds that shift and change on an ongoing basis. They move on just as your thoughts do. If you're having distressing thoughts when in pain, it sometimes helps to imagine placing those thoughts on a cloud and letting it float away.

Our thoughts are only thoughts. They aren't fixed, so they shift around and change as they do so.

8

Pain and suffering

Physical pain consists of the primary site of damage, and secondary pain, which involves the other sites around, associated with or hurting due to the primary pain. An example of primary pain is a cracked rib. The secondary pain is your sore back and stiff neck because you can't exercise, you're scared whatever movement you make will hurt and you can't sleep properly.

A consequence of the pain, especially as it becomes and remains chronic, is suffering. In a sense, suffering also has two layers. The initial layer is the suffering caused by the pain. Being in pain is tiring and distracting, and saps the enjoyment out of life. The next layer is the result of the ongoing pain and suffering, and is created over a longer period of time. It permeates many different and unexpected aspects of your life.

Suffering is the emotional and psychological distress, anger, frustration, despair and any other emotions that begin to develop as a result of chronic pain and its repercussions. These may include an inability to work, so you may struggle financially and feel useless, and disinterest in social events and friends as you feel you are no longer good company or you are unable to go on walks, play sport or sit at a table for any length of time. You may prefer not to have sexual contact or even close contact with your partner because it hurts or may hurt, so the two of you no longer cuddle or have sex, which can start to drive a wedge between you. Perhaps your mood and energy are low so you prefer to stay at home and preferably sit quietly, which can lead to feeling isolated and cut off from any pleasures in life.

These and many other situations and emotions lead to the suffering that surrounds pain, and it is this suffering that can make life feel heavy, dark and even unbearable at times. The old adage is that pain is inevitable but suffering is optional. In a somewhat simplistic way, this can be interpreted as pain comes with being alive, whether that entails physical or emotional pain, but the extent to which we let this pain influence and determine how we live our lives is where suffering comes in. We cannot always stop what happens in life when we have no control, such as an accident, a loss or an illness, but we can make a decision on how we wish to manage and deal with this situation. So, we can't stop the illness but we can choose the emotional, psychological and behavioural context – the suffering.

Chronic pain and mindfulness

Our instinct is to back away from pain when we are experiencing it or anticipate experiencing it. With mindfulness, the idea is to turn towards the pain, to reach right into it and to recognize what your experience is with this episode or moment of pain. Paradoxically, by doing this, not only do you get to recognize the variations in your experiences, but also the intensity begins to change.

If you do something and pain strikes, your brain whistles to alert your mind, thoughts and body that there is a problem. The pain becomes like a sheep that strays from the flock. Your mind starts to run around like a sheepdog looking for dangers and using all its energy and commands to get the sheep back into line. When pain strikes, your body's alarm system goes into action (the stress response), and all thoughts focus on the pain while everything else is forgotten. This aroused state takes time to settle once the pain subsides but it leaves behind a memory and fear of when it might strike again. As the pain becomes the central focus, like the runaway sheep, the rest of what you were doing or wanted to do gets delayed or put aside until later. Unsurprisingly, your pain becomes the central focus of your life.

What mindfulness can help with, with training, is developing your capacity to react to the pain in a way that gives you more control as you become able to negotiate your responses to it. What you will create within yourself by doing the meditations is the awareness and ability to do this and, most importantly, the brain networks that you can set in motion when your pain strikes. As discussed in the pain and emotional memory section in Chapter 4, a neuronal pathway – a pathway in your brain along which messages are sent (a little like a path in a forest) – develops, so the more intense or prolonged the experience, the stronger and deeper the pathway. The more you experience pain over periods of time, the more rapidly the neuronal pathways light up and the more sensitive your body becomes to pain.

It seems unfair that the more repeated pain you have, the more your body reacts to it. This happens because your brain holds the memory of painful experiences so that when you are once again in pain, your brain searches your pain memory bank at lightning speed to see if it can find a solution to your current pain situation based on past experiences. This seemingly adaptive behaviour activates your past memories, which have now been reignited as their resting place has been disturbed. It is this reactivation that sets off a chain of fear, anxiety, distress and other feelings. Your brain was not able find a solution to the current painful experience, but it did disturb a hornet's nest.

This stirring up of old memories is added to your current experience, and you may feel physically and emotionally aroused. Again, this aroused state will activate or re-engage the stress response, and this takes time to settle, which may leave you feeling tired and depressed. Even worse, the pain may never really subside, or if it does it may re-emerge soon after, once again setting off the stress response. So you have not only the physical pain, but also the emotional fallout from it, which has a tendency to spread out into the rest of your life, seriously affecting your sense of stability and quality of life. This grows and subsumes many of the once pleasurable aspects of your life, as previously outlined.

Mindfulness allows you to gain a different perspective on your pain, to create a sense of simultaneously stepping both into it and back from it. In addition, by breathing into the centre of the pain and observing it, you help to dissipate it – not to make it disappear but to soften it. The actions of stepping into the pain and breathing into it with curiosity and kindness can shift your physical and emotional tension.

The meditation practices presented in this book, particularly Body Focus, Breathe and Observe, and Mindful Awareness (the same as mindful breathing) are especially helpful in developing what has been discussed above. However, if you don't practice them on a fairly regular basis, you won't really connect with them and their benefits won't be realized. There cannot be enough emphasis on how fundamental actually doing the practices is to mindfulness, genuinely helping you to manage your pain at the point of more intense pain and manage its chronicity.

Chronic pain and suffering

There has been discussion around the effects of chronic pain that are not necessarily physical in nature – the stress, struggle and despair. This is the suffering that comes from pain. What mindfulness offers are the tools to develop your ability to step back and shift the focus, the opportunity to take control, manage your pain and ease your suffering. What is needed for this to happen is a different perspective on pain, the renegotiation of your relationship with pain and a shift in attitude towards life. By engaging in the practices, you are quietening your internal conversation and finding a deep quiet, a total presence within this moment.

Meditation is about you, your life, your pain and your joy. It is far greater than a technique or exercise, although we talk of exercising our ability to focus, concentrate and be present in order to develop a mindful mindset or approach to life. Meditation does not seek a specific mental or meditative state; it's not something abstract, disjointed or separate. In fact, it's the very opposite, in that being present, engaged and active, moment to moment, is what we aim to develop and create. Doing the practices, the formal meditations, is where the work really starts as it is this, plus the framework of a mindful attitude, that allows you to establish and connect to that quiet strength and stability within yourself.

By focusing on the task or moment of now, there is not the space or time to think of the past or future; you can't ruminate or get into other things going around in your head – the stories, regrets, fears, angers and the like. Paying attention gives you a full experience of what is happening without thoughts of other things intruding. It opens you to thinking in clearer ways when you want to think and a mode of thinking that becomes more coherent, specific and contained. You learn not to let your mind wander down dark alleys or into spirals that go into depression, fear and anxiety. Mindfulness teaches you, particularly through the practices, to label whatever is in your mind or body, such as a thought, pain or narrative, and let it drift on rather than stay with it and delve into it.

Rest your awareness on the things that happen when you focus on your breath or even on a task. Through mindfulness, you are striving for a balanced internal state. However, balance is not all positive or all negative, but a coexistence, a central point that can help you stand firm and realign during and after an intense or difficult experience of pain, or even when something good happens.

We get blocked and stuck when there is difficulty or distress. Through meditation and focused breathing, you gently shift the block and tension around it, and apply balance and care rather than a fixed negative focus on the pain. This helps you to unlatch from the suffering. The intensity of the pain may remain the same, but less mental and emotional energy goes into it, so there is less suffering associated with it.

Observe your pain with awareness and composure, which in turn allows you to see and feel the tiny changes that are happening from moment to moment. By observing your pain with this intention, you get close up to the experience you are having but you then have the opportunity and skill to step back from it. When you step back, you give yourself the space to respond to your pain in a different way, to shift the emphasis and to take control of how you negotiate it. Do you go down the dark tunnel of pain, or do you recognize the difficult, often awful, situation but see it within a context where there is you, the pain and your response to it? You use your meta-cognitive capacity, both your metacognitive knowledge and your metacognitive regulation, to do this. Knowing that you have a choice regarding how you approach and respond to your pain and suffering will empower you, but you will need to work at developing this.

Once you begin to do this, you will feel a great sense of relief knowing that you can engage with and manage your pain through getting to know it, working with it and step-ping back from it. Accept the situation, observe it and its variations, and allow a space between you and the pain, to be used by you in a way that is helpful and not destruc-tive. By not rejecting, avoiding, denying or pushing down the fact that you have chronic pain, you can come to your pain with a gentle focus, an open observation of it and the process it takes, and then apply the care, kindness and compassion that you need.

When in pain, you may feel ashamed, weak, pathetic, damned, angry, hopeless or a range of other things. By using mindfulness and its compassion, you can ride the wave of pain that emerges and its intensity, and come out without feeling as hopeless and damned. This also applies to those around you who see you in pain and feel what it can do to you and to them. Get to know your pain, its shades and variations, its locations, degrees, durations and effects – how it ebbs and flows, whether it shifts, what triggers it, what helps to ease it. Watch it and observe it with kindness and with a sense of gentle curiosity.

Resisting the pain worsens it. The fear, dismissal, avoidance, judgement and anger build up in your mind, and tension is created all over your body, setting off the stress response. You cannot help resisting the pain as this is a natural and automatic response to something unpleasant. We are geared towards survival so we look to avoid what is unpleasant, but this avoidance is not always in your best interests. The greater the resistance, the greater the suffering becomes and the more intense the pain feels, even if the actual level of pain remains the same.

The benefit of mindfulness is that it lessens your resistance, which can help you to decrease your suffering. You can lessen your resistance in your mind and body through your attitude, observing your pain, doing the formal meditations, accepting that you are in pain and will be at different points, and opening up to the pain with awareness and kindness. Your suffering decreases when you stop fighting and learn to accept and manage it.

Some may scoff at the idea of accepting your pain, but acceptance is very different from saying 'this is it, get on with it'. Pain hurts, it is pervasive, it takes over your life, but what you can do is work with it rather than fight it. Acceptance means awareness, stepping back from it and knowing it is there but not doing battle with it. Pain is the bully who wants to give you a bloody nose. Don't get into the fight – step away, observe, recognize and know the bully for who he (or she) is. Eventually, to your relief, the bully will move on and you won't have a bloody nose.

Suffering distorts your perception, interactions and behaviours as well as using up your psychological, physical and emotional energy. When you shift your energy from the fight, you have more energy to do what is helpful and even more enjoyable once the intensity of the pain subsides. This leads to an improvement in your mental state and quality of life. By opening to the pain, observing it and developing a more even mind, a greater psychological stability, composure will follow. Life is not static, and neither is your pain.

Mindfulness practice: Soles of Your Feet

This is an excellent practice that you can use at any time, such as when you are in a meeting, or on a crowded train and starting to feel agitated, if you find your anger creeping in or if you are feeling unsure of yourself. You can also do it when waiting in a doctor's reception area or sitting at home in front of the television.

- Place your feet firmly but gently on the ground. Bring your attention to the bottom of your feet, to the soles of your feet.
- Feel the sensation of your foot against your sock, your sock against the bottom of the shoe and your shoe touching the ground. If your feet are bare, feel the sensation of your bare flesh on the ground.
- Focus all of your attention on the soles of your feet.
- In your mind's eye, imagine you are breathing in and out through the soles of your feet.
- Feel each of your feet expanding and then softening with each breath.
- Imagine a sense of weight coming into your feet, a weight that is firm, strong and stabilizing.
- Let this sensation ground you as you breathe in and out.
- Bring your attention back to whatever is happening around you.

Mindfulness will give you a whole new way of managing your life in spite of feeling such pain.

9

Taking responsibility for your pain

The pattern of pain

Pain is inconsistent, and when it strikes, you forget the times when it felt easier. A difficult part of chronic pain is that it does not stay the same all day every day. You tend to have peaks and troughs at various times, but you don't always know when these will occur. Some days may feel much easier than others – you may have less pain, you feel more in control and your life seems to be going really well. Other days or times may be very different and difficult to deal with – the pain may be intense and the feelings that go with it harsh.

Consequently, you find it hard to plan ahead because you do not know how you are going to be feeling from one day to the next. Others may not understand as they may only see you at better times and not when your pain is intense. This can feel like you are on a pain rollercoaster and an emotional rollercoaster.

For this reason, it really does help to keep a pain diary – notice when you're in pain, for how long, whether something set it off, what made it worse, what helped, what did you do just before it, how did you respond to the pain, what happened next? It is surprising how keeping track helps you not only to see the peaks and troughs, but also gives you an indication of what happens, when and sometimes why.

Mindfulness practice: The Mountain Meditation

The Mountain Meditation is designed to create a sense of stability, balance and well-being. It is about claiming this moment and this space for yourself, and anchoring yourself no matter how distressing life may be. It is a reminder of your personal resilience, reassuring you that you can weather any storm, even in the face of pain. If you can't stand up for this practice, sit in a chair or prop yourself up in bed.

🔊 Listen to the Mountain Meditation track. Once you've completed the track, think about how you face difficulties, the storms you have weathered and the times you thought you could not cope or that life was not going to get better. Hold in your mind what you think helped you to get through it.

Below is a transcript of the Mountain Meditation practice, which you can find on the audio download.

Transcript of the Mountain Meditation practice

Stand with your feet hip width apart so that you can balance yourself. Keep your knees soft and your hips loose, imagining there is a small weight attached to your tailbone (coccyx). Tuck your navel in towards your spine as though you are pulling in your stomach to tighten your belt. Relax your shoulders into your back, lightly tuck in your chin, and let your head balance on top of your spine. Breathe in, and on an outbreath let unwanted tension be released. On an inbreath, take in a feeling of relaxed strength.

As you stand, be aware of your breath moving in at the nostrils, down the back of the throat, into the chest and down into the abdomen, and then its movement from the abdomen, through the chest and throat, and out through the nose. Allow a natural rhythm of breathing, not forcing the breath in or out in any way.

While standing here, feel the weight of your body in your feet, firm against the earth, and that the earth can carry your weight with confidence. Let your breath feel as if it is moving all the way down into your feet, giving them strength and stability. Now let the breath move into your ankles, strengthening them, and now into the calves. Let it flow into your knees, without locking them, and then into your thighs. Move the breath and steadiness into your hips, genitals, buttocks and abdomen, and let this area of your body feel strong but relaxed.

Allow the breath and strength to move up your spine at the back, through your stomach and chest, eventually reaching your shoulders, checking that they are relaxed. Your arms becoming stronger and part of the mountain, stabilizing you, balancing you. Let it move into your neck and jaw, into the skull, ears, face, eyes and right up to the top of your head.

Now, in your mind's eye, move the breath to the base of your spine and thread it like a piece of string through each vertebra from the tailbone, up through the pelvis, the lower back, the middle of your back, the shoulder blade area, the back of the neck and all the way to the top of your head where it exits and is held gently but firmly on a hook, allowing your body to hold itself.

Feel the sensation of this, of your body standing like a mountain, fixed and firm, gracious and solid. The mountain is stable and grand: the earth beneath it, the sky and air around it. The weather changes, the seasons move from one to another, but the mountain remains. Feel the strength of the earth beneath you, solid and powerful, and your body open and alert, as you stand grounded and dignified in this space.

No matter how chaotic life may seem at times, you already have coping skills that you use on a daily basis and in more stressful situations. Now you can build and develop even more resilience. Find that one thing within yourself, no matter how small, that you know is strong and firm and remind yourself of it each day.

Thoughts, emotions and experiences are transient, but the core of you is constant and enduring. By engaging in practices such as the Mountain Meditation, you are reinforcing your capacity to choose wellness over distress. Mindfulness is as much about celebrating your achievements, success and health as it is about negotiating the more difficult or negative experiences of your life.

Centring on the present moment can increase your understanding of what has happened in the past, and better your chances of a calmer, more grounded future.

Pain triggers

Your pain diary can help you to know what situations or activities induce your pain or aggravate it. Doing too much or too little, your mood, an argument, a disappointment, the temperature or repeating the same movements may trigger your pain.

Sometimes your body will do certain things before a flare-up occurs, or the pain triggers may not be controllable; use these signs to start doing something to modify their impact, such as a mindfulness practice. You may have found some mindfulness practices easier depending on the intensity of your pain, or you may have a preference for a particular one. It will be useful for you to know which practices help you cope with a flare-up the most.

Being sensible

Pacing yourself is essential because it is so easy when you are not in pain to want to make up for lost time. The consequence is that if you do too much, you will have a setback. You need to prioritize the requirements of your life and take time off before an incident has been triggered. However, what you do not want is to take it so easy that you start to feel isolated, bored and cut off from the world and others. This can lead to depression so it is necessary to keep some social interaction and activity on the go.

Take breaks, plan things, get organized, be realistic and be sensible. Get enough sleep, eat well, talk to others, exercise, set goals for each day, even if that entails needing to stay indoors or resting. Don't step away from life. Know which areas of your life are out of balance and put things in place, one thing at a time, to ease the strain. For example, if you find ironing very difficult, get someone in to do it or delegate the task. There is no point pushing yourself to do it if it sets off pain. You also need to manage your expectations of yourself and others because if they are unrealistic, that can readily lead to friction and disapproval of them and of yourself.

Setting boundaries is also very important because they help to protect you, help your pain management and give you the opportunity to take time to do things such as the meditations or other helpful interventions. Something as simple as saying 'I'm going to sit in the garden on my own and have a cup of tea' is setting a boundary.

Sleep

Sleep is essential to your well-being and sanity. Pain often interrupts sleep, so this is an area that you need to address. In brief, doing a short breathing practice just before bedtime or when you wake up during the night can help. If you wake up and are still in a state of drowsiness, it sometimes helps to focus on your breathing – you can count or say 'in' on an inbreath and 'out' on an outbreath. You may fall asleep again without realizing it.

Another approach is to acknowledge to yourself what-ever is on your mind and then tell yourself that there isn't anything you can do about it at this given moment (e.g. 3.00 a.m.). Agree with yourself to put it aside (imagine placing it on the bedside table or floor) until the morning.

Alternatively, if it is a conversation in your head or you are going over an old happening, say to yourself that you need to stop going over it for now as you have been over it many times before, and right now it is important that you rest your mind and body. Going over it again, at this moment, is not going to make any difference. You can tell yourself that you can go over it as many times as you want in the morning, but now is for sleeping. The aim is not to try and force yourself to stop whatever is going on but to recognize it, negotiate with yourself to put it aside for now and then give yourself permission to go to sleep or back to sleep.

If you can't sleep over a long period of time, it is best to get up and do something. This should not be anything that activates your brain, such as sitting at your computer or reading on your phone. Watching TV also may not be helpful as it has sound and moving images. Some people may become overly stimulated by it, whereas others may fall asleep in front of the television set but then have to wake up as they are uncomfortable, are still sitting up or are in pain. Watching TV in bed is definitely not good. It is better to watch it in another room as your bedroom should be a place that you associate with sleep and quiet.

If you must get up, read, make a cup of tea, tidy a drawer – the aim is to use up some of the mental energy that is stopping you from sleeping until you are in a better frame of mind to return to bed. Read a magazine, switch on the radio or listen to music if you are unable to get up on your own. Use headphones if you need to.

An important issue is to prepare yourself for sleep before becoming drowsy. Our bodies work in cycles, so if you feel drowsy and then get up, brush your teeth and so forth, you will be awake again by the time you get into bed. Be ready so that you can go straight to bed and you will fall asleep. If you do need to get out of bed because you cannot sleep or have awoken, then go back to bed as soon as you start to feel drowsy once more. You must learn to listen to your body cycle and go to sleep or get back into bed straight away.

Journals

A journal of your events and experiences is a very helpful way of taking things out of your head and giving them some perspective. It allows you to keep track of what is happening and how you are responding to situations. Writing can let us be honest with ourselves and bring random thoughts or anxieties to the fore, which can then be expressed in a clearer and more contained way.

When pain hits

Unfortunately, no matter how sensible you are being, there will be episodes beyond your control. Acknowledge what is happening and do the right thing. Think about what has been said about pain and suffering, and how you can approach this episode or flare-up from a mindful stance. Act on the pain by using and doing whatever helps you, including perhaps a short practice. Keep altering your position, and gently stretch and rotate your limbs and joints to prevent becoming too stiff and in a worse situation.

Remind yourself that things will start to improve and you will therefore not allow it to play a role in any more suffering that will delay your recovery. Reinforce for yourself that you are doing the best you can at this point and that that's all you should be doing.

Hold on to the good times: during periods of intense pain, time may seem to drag and everything can seem insurmountable and impossible. It is therefore useful to reflect on activities that you may have been doing a few days ago, a week ago or when the pain was less intense. This can help you to restore a more realistic perspective of time and reassure you that you will be able to get through this and return to doing those activities. Don't let yourself get into the spiral of catastrophizing what is happening. Your pain will shift; the intensity will ease.

In the midst of a spell of intense pain, you may not be able to think of or work out any effective alternative coping strategies, so it is important to work out a plan in advance. Having a plan to turn to means that you will feel assured that you are in control of the situation. The very process of preparing and writing down how you can self-manage your everyday pain and the periods of flare-up pain will instil faith and confidence that you will cope and get through the challenging periods.

The plan needs to be what works for you and your pain. It should be comprehensive and detailed so that someone else can clearly interpret it and understand what you need to do and what they need to do during a pain flare-up. Keep a copy somewhere in plain sight so that it acts as a reminder and helps you take back control when things begin to slide. Bear in mind, however, that the same strategy may not work every time, so you may need to build in flexibility and adapt the plan accordingly. At the start of a flare-up, a certain technique or practice may not make much of a difference to the way you are feeling, but it may transform things a little later in the day.

You may also find it reassuring to have a flare-up 'safety box' so that you can have things at hand as soon as an episode starts. Keep the box somewhere that is accessible to keep the items at hand. It can contain anything you need access to at short notice and will prevent you from feeling anxious about finding these items, especially if the pain hits quickly. It might contain a copy of your favourite book, a recording of the meditations on a device that you can use, a friend's or support person's phone number, an emergency number, a pillow or body rest, some medications, a hot water bottle or cool pack, a bar of chocolate, a soft blanket and a plastic dish in case you feel sick.

Scepticism is fine

Being unsure about this new approach is to be expected. No doubt you have in the past tried things that have promised to help but haven't. With mindfulness, the benefits come from both your approach and continuing to do the practices – without them, it's like taking half your dose of medication and then wondering why it's not helping, or stopping it because you think it's ineffective. Mindfulness isn't just for today or this week; it's a resource that you develop within yourself with each observation, with each practice, with each experience. It becomes your anchor that you can drop when the seas get rough or you simply want to remain calm and steady in shifting times.

Mindfulness is an ongoing process that happens gradually. It takes time, effort, trial and error and ongoing engagement. It takes a willingness to be open to a different experience, to a way of observing your pain and other aspects of your life without any specific purpose other than to observe and be open, with kindness. Through this, your relationship to your pain and yourself will begin to shift.

Every day should involve a practice, no matter how short – a few mindful moments, the Body Focus, a five-minute meditation, a mindful snack or a 20-minute mindful awareness practice. All the practices are based on awareness, opening and observing. They are all about focusing on the present, using your breath and observing what is happening, even if it's nothing. The more you do this, the more you will want to do it and the more frequently occasions will occur where mindfulness has benefited you and the management of your pain.

Here you are being offered a new way to approach your pain; life is both wonderful and difficult, all at the same time. The aim of mindfulness is to help you manage all of your experiences, even ones that do not involve pain. It can become part of you, and once you start to face its challenges and achievements you can truly embrace it in your life.

Find a way that makes it work **for** *you not* **against** *you.*

10

Life with pain, life without suffering

Keep your perspective

You may be feeling that you are defined by the problems you've been struggling with, but that is not true. You are you because of all your experiences, and each part of you needs to learn to coexist with the other parts, to live together without trying to avoid or deny one set in favour of others. You can gradually develop your ability to care about all of yourself, as you are now, and to appreciate your present moment for all that you are, even if you view some of it as flawed.

Keeping perspective can switch your mindset from a negative, despondent one to a more accepting and open one. It's quite easy to lose balance and to see one incident or experience as the only issue of concern. This can distort and dismiss the other aspects of your life and be harmful to your own well-being and that of others.

If you lose perspective, you lose your equanimity, your balance in life.

Gratitude

Gratitude may seem a strange concept to raise within the context of pain. Naturally, it's not about you being grateful for your condition, but about keeping perspective so that you can still recognize the good that you have. Gratitude can lead to an increase in determination, attention, enthusiasm and energy[1,2] in adults and adolescents. It has a direct impact for people with chronic pain in terms of improved sleep and decreased levels of depression, with the improved sleep lessening anxiety.[3] Gratitude is not only strongly correlated with well-being, but also has the potential to improve well-being through practising it.[4] Gracefully being aware of, and acknowledging, what you have in your life is a powerful antidote to distress.

Life is not perfect, and for many reading this book there are probably aspects of it that strike at your very core. But there is seldom nothing in life that one cannot feel some sense of gratitude about, even when facing a terminal illness. Gratitude is about finding value in life and respecting that which is good, no matter how small – a smile, a warm bed, a kind friend. Gratitude helps you to be attuned to the nuances of life and be thankful for those that bring you comfort, pleasure or greater understanding.

When you view your life through eyes that notice all of life, the good and the harsh, and you feel a sense of thankfulness for the good, no matter how small, it helps you to keep perspective – a smile from a stranger, laughter with a friend or food in your stomach. Accepting the transience of your life and its situations, and knowing that what you have in this moment is the most important thing, allows you to feel gratitude. Each night before you go to sleep, think of at least two things from your day for which you are grateful.

Compassion and kindness

Coupled with gratitude is compassion, a feeling and showing of tenderness and softness towards suffering, particularly your own suffering. You may feel uneasy showing kindness and compassion to yourself as you may not think you deserve it, or may feel that it is something that you give to others and not to yourself. You may feel ashamed about your condition and so not believe you are worthy of them. Perhaps you will need to learn how to give yourself this gentleness and care, because without it life can feel very harsh.

Being in pain means that you probably cannot do all that you would like to or had anticipated. It could mean less intimacy, fewer social interactions, not working, relying on others to manage financially and more. Without self-compassion, there is too much room for self-criticism, judgement and self-hate. Compassion is the shoulder upon which you can lean so that you can reach your destination. Without it, getting through each day can seem like a battleground, and when your pain flares up or you are going through a difficult time, being compassionate and loving towards yourself will give you strength, endurance and nurturance.

Self-care meditation

Mindfulness practice: Self-care and Compassion Meditation

This meditation is a starting point for developing a kind and caring attitude towards yourself. Sit quietly in any position that is comfortable for you and take a few mindful breaths. Repeat the following phrases to yourself:

- May I be happy and healthy.
- May I accept myself for all that I am.
- May I live my life with ease.

Repeat these phrases a number of times, even when it feels difficult. When we are anxious or depressed, we can start to doubt that we are worthy of love or that we deserve to be happy. However, these are just thoughts; we do not need to latch on to them. Everyone is deserving of love and happiness, and you can start to cultivate a sense of kindness and care towards yourself. You can change the wording to suit your own ideas of generosity, kindness and care towards yourself.

Life without suffering

We suffer because we are human beings capable of it. Our suffering can help us to be understanding and empathic of others and what happens in their lives. However, when we attach ourselves so strongly to our expectations of life, people and outcomes, we run the risk of being disappointed and disgruntled. The 'if only' scenario plays through our minds, and what we actually do have gets lost, forgotten about or pushed aside as insufficient. When we can manage our lives and separate them from the suffering that we attach to our experiences, we can begin to focus on all that we do have, even when it involves pain. The pain comes and goes, life comes and goes, but what remains constant is the realness of this moment for all that it brings. Be gentle and kind to yourself as each moment unfolds and passes.

You will notice that the more you do the practices, the greater the benefits. One of these benefits is that you can readily learn how to refocus your attention. Throughout the book and in the practices, there are a number of references to coming back to your anchor, to that part within you that is stable and balanced. When life is busy, when things get tough or distressing, when fear arises or you're feeling adrift, *drop anchor*. Make the association in your mind of that anchor always being there to ground you, to help keep you steadfast and allow for equanimity, for calm and balance in the midst of shifting times.

Live your life one breath at a time.

Notes

1 Pain in perspective

1 National Pain Audit – <www.nationalpainaudit.org/media/files/NationalPainAudit-2012.pdf>.
2 Pain UK – <https://painuk.org/>.
3 Office of National Statistics (2014), *Sickness Absence in the Labour Market*, London: ONS.
4 Health & Safety Executive (2016), *Labour Force Survey 2015*, Liverpool: HSE.
5 University College London, School of Pharmacy (2012), *Relieving Persistent Pain: Improving Health Outcomes*, London: UCL.
6 American Academy of Pain Medicine – <www.painmed.org>.
7 Hoy, D., March. L., Brooks, P. et al. (2014), 'The Global Burden of Low Back Pain: Estimates from the Global Burden of Disease 2010 Study'. *Annals of Rheumatic Disease* 73(6), pp. 968–74.
8 Nair, S., Sagar, M., Sollers, J., Consedine, N. and Broadbent, E. (2015), 'Do Slumped and Upright Postures Affect Stress Responses? A Randomized Trial'. *Health Psychology* 34(6), pp. 632–41.

2 The different angles of pain

1 University College London, School of Pharmacy (2012), *Relieving Persistent Pain: Improving Health Outcomes*, London: UCL.
2 NHS Choices – <www.nhs.uk/conditions/medically-unexplained-symptoms/pages/somatisation.aspx>.
3 Melzack, R. and Wall P. D. (1965), 'Pain Mechanisms: A New Theory'. *Science* 150(3699), pp. 971–9.
4 Derbyshire NHS Trust, Health Psychology Service (2012), *The Gate Control Theory*.

5 Free, M. M. (2002), 'Cross-cultural Conceptions of Pain and Pain Control'. *Proceedings (Baylor University Medical Center)* 15(2), pp. 143–5.

6 Hart, R. P., Wade, J. B. and Martelli, M. F. (2003), 'Cognitive Impairment in Patients with Chronic Pain: The Significance of Stress'. *Current Pain and Headache Reports* 7(2), pp. 116–26.

7 Moriarty, O., McGuire, B. E. and Finn, D. P. (2011), 'The Effect of Pain on Cognitive Function. A Review of Clinical and Preclinical Research'. *Progress in Neurobiology* 93(3), pp. 385–404.

8 Naylor, C., Parsonage, M., McDavid, D. et al. (2012), *Longterm Conditions and Mental Health: The Cost of Co-morbidity*, London: Kings Fund.

9 Pazzanese, C. (2015), 'Matching Policy to Power of Addiction'. *Harvard Gazette*, 6 October.

10 Cicero, T., Ellis, M., Surratt, H. and Kurtz, S. (2014), 'The Changing Face of Heroin Use in the United States: A Retrospective Analysis of the Past 50 Years'. *JAMA Psychiatry* 71(7), p. 8216.

11 Wiesenfeld-Hallin, Z. (2005), 'Sex Differences in Pain Perception'. *Gender Medicine* 2(3), pp. 137–45.

12 Rezek, C. (2011), 'The Different Angles of Pain'. *Pain News*, Summer, pp. 29–31 – <www.lifehappens-mindfulness.com/wp-content /uploads/2013/02/The-Different-Angles-of-Pain-enc_painarticle. pdf>.

13 Zeidan, F., Emerson, N., Farris, S. et al. (2015), 'Mindfulness Meditation-based Pain Relief Employs Different Neural Mechanisms than Placebo and Sham Mindfulness Meditation-induced Analgesia'. *Journal of Neuroscience* 35(46), pp. 15307–25.

14 Cherkin, D. C., Sherman, K. J., Balderson, B. H. et al. (2016), 'Effect of Mindfulness-based Stress Reduction vs Cognitive Behavioral Therapy or Usual Care on Back Pain and Functional Limitations in Adults with Chronic Low Back Pain: A Randomized Clinical Trial'. *Journal of the American Medical Association* 315(12), pp. 1240–9.

3 Mindfulness and pain

1 Allen, N. B., Chambers, R., Knight, W.; Melbourne Academic Mindfulness Interest Group (2006), 'Mindfulness-based Psychotherapies: A Review of Conceptual Foundations, Empirical Evidence and Practical Considerations'. *Australian and New Zealand Journal of Psychiatry* 40(4), pp. 285–94.

2 Baker, L. (2016), Metacognition – <www.education.com/reference /article/metacognition/>.

3 Cusens, B., Duggan, G. B., Thorne, K. et al. (2010), 'Evaluation of the Breathworks Mindfulness-based Pain Management Programme: Effects on Well-being and Multiple Measures of Mindfulness'. *Clinical Psychology and Psychotherapy* 17(1), pp. 63–78.

4 Dowd, H., Hogan, M. J., McGuire, B. E. et al. (2015), 'Comparison of an Online Mindfulness-based Cognitive Therapy Intervention with Online Pain Management Psychoeducation: A Randomized Controlled Study'. *Clinical Journal of Pain* 31(6), pp. 517–27.

5 Donatone, B. (2013), 'Focused Suggestion with Somatic Anchoring Technique: Rapid Self-hypnosis for Pain Management'. *American Journal of Clinical Hypnosis* 55(4), pp. 325–42.

6 Zeidan, F., Grant, J. A., Brown, C. A. et al. (2012), 'Mindfulness Meditation-related Pain Relief: Evidence for Unique Brain Mechanisms in the Regulation of Pain'. *Neuroscience Letters* 520(2), pp. 165–73.

7 Zeidan, F., Martucci, K. T., Kraft, R. A. et al. (2011), 'Brain Mechanisms Supporting the Modulation of Pain by Mindfulness Meditation'. *Journal of Neuroscience* 31(14), pp. 5540–8.

8 Gard, T., Holzel, B. K., Sack, A. T. et al. (2012), 'Pain Attenuation Through Mindfulness is Associated with Decreased Cognitive Control and Increased Sensory Processing in the Brain'. *Cerebral Cortex* 22(11), pp. 2692–702.

9 Cho, S. K., Heiby, E. M., McCracken, L. M. et al. (2010), 'Pain-related Anxiety as a Mediator of the Effects of Mindfulness on Physical and Psychosocial Functioning in Chronic Pain Patients in Korea'. *Journal of Pain* 11(8), pp. 789–97.

10 McCracken, L. M. and Keogh, E. (2009), 'Acceptance, Mind-

fulness, and Values-based Action May Counteract Fear and Avoidance of Emotions in Chronic Pain: An Analysis of Anxiety Sensitivity'. *Journal of Pain* 10(4), pp. 408–15.

11 Ussher, M., Spatz, A., Copland, C. et al. (2014), 'Immediate Effects of a Brief Mindfulness-based Body Scan on Patients with Chronic Pain'. *Journal of Behavioural Medicine* 37(1), pp. 127–34.

12 Cassidy, E. L., Atherton, R. J., Robertson, N. et al, (2012), 'Mindfulness, Functioning and Catastrophizing after Multidisciplinary Pain Management for Chronic Low Back Pain'. *Pain* 153(3), pp. 644–50.

13 Esmer, G., Blum, J., Rulf, J. and Pier, J. (2010), 'Mindfulness-based Stress Reduction for Failed Back Surgery Syndrome: A Randomized Controlled Trial'. *Journal of the American Osteopathic Association* 110(11), pp. 646–52.

14 Beaulac, J. and Bailly, M. (2015), 'Mindfulness-Based Stress Reduction: Pilot Study of a Treatment Group for Patients with Chronic Pain in a Primary Care Setting'. *Primary Health Care Research and Development* 16(4), pp. 424–8.

15 Wong, S. Y., Chan, F. W., Wong, R. L. et al. (2011), 'Comparing the Effectiveness of Mindfulness-based Stress Reduction and Multidisciplinary Intervention Programs for Chronic Pain: A Randomized Comparative Trial'. *Clinical Journal of Pain* 27(8), pp. 724–34.

16 Weber, B., Jermann, F., Lutz, A. et al. (2012), 'Mindfulness-based Therapeutic Approaches: Benefits for Individuals Suffering from Pain'. *Revue Medicale Suisse* 8(347), pp. 1395–8.

17 LaCour, P. and Petersen, M. (2015), 'Effects of Mindfulness Meditation on Chronic Pain: A Randomized Controlled Trial'. *Pain Medicine* 16(4), pp. 641–52.

18 Gardner-Nix, J., Backman, S., Barbati, J. et al. (2008), 'Evaluating Distance Education of a Mindfulness-based Meditation Programme for Chronic Pain Management'. *Journal of Telemedicine and Telecare* 14(2), pp. 88–92.

19 Garland, E. L. (2014), 'Disrupting the Downward Spiral of Chronic Pain and Opioid Addiction with Mindfulness-oriented Recovery Enhancement: A Review of Clinical Outcomes and

Neurocognitive Targets'. *Journal of Pain and Palliative Care Pharmacotherapy* 28(2), pp. 122–9.

20 Reiner, K., Tibi, L. and Lipsitz, J. D. (2013), 'Do Mindfulness-based Interventions Reduce Pain Intensity? A Critical Review of the Literature'. *Pain Medicine* 14(2), pp. 230–42.

21 Petter, M., McGrath, P. J., Chambers, C. T. et al. (2014), 'The Effects of Mindful Attention and State Mindfulness on Acute Experimental Pain Among Adolescents'. *Journal of Pediatric Psychology* 39(5), pp. 521–31.

22 Prins, B., Decuypere, A., Van Damme, S. (2014), 'Effects of Mindfulness and Distraction on Pain Depend upon Individual Differences in Pain Catastrophizing: An Experimental Study'. *European Journal of Pain* 18(9), pp. 1307–15.

23 Liu, X., Wang, S., Chang, S. et al. (2013), 'Effect of Brief Mindfulness Intervention on Tolerance and Distress of Pain Induced by Cold-pressor Task'. *Stress and Health* 29(3), pp. 199–204.

24 Schutze, R., Slater, H., O'Sullivan, P. et al. (2014), 'Mindfulness-Based Functional Therapy: A Preliminary Open Trial of an Integrated Model of Care for People with Persistent Low Back Pain'. *Frontiers in Psychology* 5, p. 839.

25 Doran, N. J. (2014), 'Experiencing Wellness Within Illness: Exploring a Mindfulness-based Approach to Chronic Back Pain'. *Qualitative Health Research* 24(6), pp. 749–60.

26 Banth, S. and Ardebil, M. D. (2015), 'Effectiveness of Mindfulness Meditation on Pain and Quality of Life of Patients with Chronic Low Back Pain'. *International Journal of Yoga* 8(2), pp. 128–33.

27 Morone, N., Greco, C., Weiner, D. K. (2008), 'Mindfulness Meditation for the Treatment of Chronic Low Back Pain in Older Adults: A Randomized Controlled Pilot Study'. *Pain* 134(3), pp. 310–19.

28 Kold, M., Hansen, T., Vedsted-Hansen, H. et al. (2012), 'Mindfulness-based Psychological Intervention for Coping with Pain in Endometriosis'. *Nordic Psychology* 64(1), pp. 2–16.

29 Davis, M. C., Zautra, A. J., Wolf, L. D. et al. (2015), 'Mindfulness and Cognitive-behavioral Interventions for Chronic Pain:

Differential Effects on Daily Pain Reactivity and Stress Reactivity'. *Journal of Consulting and Clinical Psychology* 83(1), pp. 24–35.

30 Oberg, E. B., Rempe, M. and Bradley, R. (2013), 'Self-directed Mindfulness Training and Improvement in Blood Pressure, Migraine Frequency, and Quality of Life'. *Global Advances in Health and Medicine* 2(2), pp. 20–5.

31 Wells, R. E., Burch, R., Paulsen, R. H. et al. (2014), 'Meditation for Migraines: A Pilot Randomized Controlled Trial'. *Headache* 54(9), pp. 1484–95.

32 Cathcart, S., Galatis, N., Immink, M. et al. (2014), 'Brief Mindfulness-based Therapy for Chronic Tension-Type Headache: A Randomized Controlled Pilot Study'. *Behavioral and Cognitive Psychotherapy* 42(1), pp. 1–15.

33 Day, M. A., Thorn, B. E., Ward, L. C. et al. (2014), 'Mindfulness-based Cognitive Therapy for the Treatment of Headache Pain: A Pilot Study'. *Clinical Journal of Pain* 30(2), pp. 152–61.

34 Bakhshani, N. M., Amirani, A., Amirifard, H. et al. (2015), 'The Effectiveness of Mindfulness-based stress Reduction on Perceived Pain Intensity and Quality of Life in Patients with Chronic Headache'. *Global Journal of Health Science* 8(4), pp. 142–51.

35 Song, Y., Lu, H., Chen, H. et al. (2014), 'Mindfulness Intervention in the Management of Chronic Pain and Psychological Co-morbidity: A Meta-analysis'. *International Journal of Nursing Sciences* 1(2), pp. 215–23.

36 Dowd, H., Hogan, M. J., McGuire, B. E. et al. (2015), 'Comparison of an Online Mindfulness-based Cognitive Therapy Intervention with Online Pain Management Psychoeducation: A Randomized Controlled Study'. *Clinical Journal of Pain* 31(6), pp. 517–27.

37 McCracken, L. M. and Gauntlett-Gilbert, J. (2011), 'Role of Psychological Flexibility in Parents of Adolescents with Chronic Pain: Development of a Measure and Preliminary Correlation Analyses'. *Pain* 152(4), pp. 780–5.

38 Petter, M., Chambers, C. T. and MacLaren Chorney, J. (2013), 'The Effects of Mindfulness-based Attention on Cold Pressor Pain in Children'. *Pain Research and Management* 18(1), pp. 39–45.

4 My mind or my body

1 National Pain Audit – <www.nationalpainaudit.org/media/files/ NationalPainAudit-2012.pdf>.

2 Woolf, C. (2011), 'Central Sensitization: Implications for the Diagnosis and Treatment of Pain'. *Pain* 152(3 Suppl), pp. S2–15.

3 Rezek, C. A. (2003), *Avoidance of Traumatic Memories in Depressed, Never Depressed and Recovered Individuals*, Doctoral Thesis, City University, London.

4 Rezek, C. A. (2010), *Life Happens: Waking up to Yourself and Your Life in a Mindful Way*, London: Leachcroft.

6 Pain and movement

1 NHS Choices – <www.nhs.uk/conditions/stress-anxiety-depression/pages/stress-relief-exercise.aspx>.

7 Mindful awareness – mindful breathing

1 Davidson, R. J., Kabat-Zinn, J., Schumacher, J. et al. (2003), 'Alterations in Brain and Immune Function Produced by Mindfulness Meditation'. *Psychosomatic Medicine* 65(4), pp. 564–70.

2 Hölzel, B. K., Carmody, J., Vangel, M. et al. (2011), 'Mindfulness Practice Leads to Increases in Regional Brain Gray Matter Density'. *Psychiatry Research: Neuroimaging* 191(1), pp. 36–43.

3 Coffey, K. A., Hartman, M. and Fredrickson, B. L. (2010), 'Deconstructing Mindfulness and Constructing Mental Health: Understanding Mindfulness and its Mechanisms of Action'. *Mindfulness* 1(4), pp. 235–53.

4 Pressley, M., Wood, E., Woloshyn, V. E. et al. (1992), 'Encouraging Mindful Use of Prior Knowledge: Attempting to Construct Explanatory Answers Facilitates Learning'. *Educational Psychologist* 27(1), pp. 91–109.

5 Heeren, A., Van Broeck, N. and Philippot, P. (2009), 'The Effects of Mindfulness on Executive Processes and Autobiographical Memory Specificity'. *Behaviour Research and Therapy* 47(5), pp. 403–9.

6 Brown, K. W. and Ryan, R. M. (2003), 'The Benefits of Being

Present: Mindfulness and its Role in Psychological Well-being'. *Journal of Personality and Social Psychology* 84(4), p. 822.

7   Allen, N. B., Chambers, R., Knight, W.; Academic Mindfulness Interest Group (2006), 'Mindfulness-based Psychotherapies: A Review of Conceptual Foundations, Empirical Evidence and Practical Considerations'. *Australian and New Zealand Journal of Psychiatry* 40(4), pp. 285–94.

8   Cresswell, D. J., Taren, A. D., Lindsay, E. K. et al. (2016), 'Alterations in Resting State Functional Connectivity Link Mindfulness Meditation with Reduced Interleukin-6: A Randomized Controlled Trial'. *Biological Psychiatry* 80(1), pp. 53–61.

9   Sanders, R. (2011), 'New Evidence that Chronic Stress Predisposes Brain to Mental Illness' – <news.berkeley.edu/2014/02/11/chronic -stress-predisposes-brain-to-mental-illness/>.

10 Zeidan, F., Emerson, N., Farris, S. et al. (2015), 'Mindfulness Meditation-based Pain Relief Employs Different Neural Mechanisms than Placebo and Sham Mindfulness Meditation-induced Analgesia'. *Journal of Neuroscience* 35(46), pp. 15307–25.

10 Life without pain, life without suffering

1   Emmons, R. A. and CcCullough, M. E. (2003), 'Counting Blessings Versus Burdens: An Experimental Investigation of Gratitude and Subjective Well-being in Daily Life'. *Journal of Personality and Social Psychology* 84(2), pp. 377–89.

2   Froh, J. J., Sefick, W. J. and Emmons, R. A. (2008), 'Counting Blessings in Early Adolescents: An Experimental Study of Gratitude and Subjective Well-being'. *Journal of School Psychology* 46(2), pp. 213–33.

3   Ng, M. and Wong, W. (2013), 'The Differential Effects of Gratitude and Sleep on Psychological Distress in Patients with Chronic Pain'. *Journal of Health Psychology* 18(2), pp. 263–71.

4   Wood, A. M., Froh, J. J. and Geraghty, A. W. (2010), 'Gratitude and Well-being: A Review and Theoretical Integration'. *Clinical Psychology Review* 30(7), pp. 890–905.